Rescued
by Angels

First published by O Books, 2009
O Books is an imprint of John Hunt Publishing Ltd., The Bothy, Deershot Lodge, Park Lane, Ropley,
Hants, SO24 0BE, UK
office1@o-books.net
www.o-books.net

Distribution in:	South Africa
	Alternative Books
UK and Europe	altbook@peterhyde.co.za
Orca Book Services	Tel: 021 555 4027 Fax: 021 447 1430
orders@orcabookservices.co.uk	
Tel: 01202 665432 Fax: 01202 666219	Text copyright Philippa Merivale 2008
Int. code (44)	
	Design: Stuart Davies
USA and Canada	
NBN	ISBN: 978 1 84694 175 7
custserv@nbnbooks.com	
Tel: 1 800 462 6420 Fax: 1 800 338 4550	All rights reserved. Except for brief quotations
	in critical articles or reviews, no part of this
Australia and New Zealand	book may be reproduced in any manner without
Brumby Books	prior written permission from the publishers.
sales@brumbybooks.com.au	
Tel: 61 3 9761 5535 Fax: 61 3 9761 7095	The rights of Philippa Merivale as author have
	been asserted in accordance with the
Far East (offices in Singapore, Thailand,	Copyright, Designs and Patents Act 1988.
Hong Kong, Taiwan)	
Pansing Distribution Pte Ltd	
kemal@pansing.com	A CIP catalogue record for this book is available
Tel: 65 6319 9939 Fax: 65 6462 5761	from the British Library.

Printed by Digital Book Print

O Books operates a distinctive and ethical publishing philosophy in
all areas of its business, from its global network of authors to
production and worldwide distribution.
This book is produced on FSC certified stock, within ISO14001
standards. The printer plants sufficient trees each year through
the Woodland Trust to absorb the level of emitted carbon in
its production.

Rescued
by Angels

Philippa Merivale

BOOKS

Winchester, UK
Washington, USA

CONTENTS

Reviews

Healing has always been considered a divine gift, and healers have always existed in every culture on earth. Rescued By Angels is a riveting story of real-life healing that will bring hope and inspiration to all who read it. My advice: buy two copies – *one for you and one for your physician.*

Larry Dossey, MD

Author: HEALING WORDS and THE POWER OF PREMONITIONS

This is one of those self-help books which belongs in every person's home and community library for constant reference. While it reads like the most gripping of novels, as riveting and informative and inspiring and entertaining as any I've read, it's the best of courses in achieving happy reality for the most challenged, for everyone.

Suzanne Mendelssohn, Ph.D.

Chairperson, Global Comm. on Exceptional Healing, Univ. of Arizona

Powerful, enlightening and uplifting, Rescued by Angels reminds us that so much of life is about trust, about dancing with the fears we face in adversity, and about doing our best to ensure that our 'story' ceases to be one that allows us to stay wedded to the 'victim' stance.

An inspirational narrative of personal and universal healing that will strike a chord with absolutely anybody who reads it.

Max Eames

Psychotherapist and Author of WEALTH MECHANIC

Philippa Merivale is a teacher's teacher. Through courage and faith she has transformed one of life's greatest challenges...the near-fatal accident of her daughter. Rescued by Angels is an amazing account and awakening into Metatronic Healing. The true power of this work lies in the reality of her child Magdalen's journey back to life. I highly recommend this book, in fact it just may save your life.

Dr Darren Weissman

Developer of The LifeLine Technique

Author of THE POWER OF INFINITE LOVE & GRATITUDE

For all the Angels and Wizards in my life.
And all the floaty people too.

FOREWORD

"If you came this way,
Taking any route, starting from anywhere,
At any time or at any season,
It would always be the same: you would have to put off
Sense and notion. You are not here to verify,
Instruct yourself, or inform curiosity
Or carry report. You are here to kneel
Where prayer has been valid."
T.S. Eliot. Little Gidding.

These words by T.S. Eliot have rung true for me ever since I first read them as a child, pinned up on the wall of my mother's studio. I would marvel at them, written in her beautiful calligraphy, not knowing what they meant, yet somehow touched inwardly by their resonance and rhythm. Gradually their significance dawned on me. I cannot remember when first they became meaningful and true – but they did. In like manner I know that Philippa Merivale could not tell me at what moment the import of the rhythm and meaning of her life dawned on her – but it did. It is written in this book.

This is a true story – every word of it, every nuance, every breath, every heartbeat, every moment. Read it. Feel it. Think it. Visualise it. See it. Imagine it. Ponder it – and in so doing wonder about the fact, the truism that "the truth is often stranger than fiction". I doubt any one could have dreamed up this story. And yet, of course, the truth that Philippa Merivale tells is that she did dream up the story that is her life – no one else dreamed that particular dream – only she did. And that is the fundamental truth that underpins this remarkable autobiography. It is woven through every nuance, every warp and weft of the magic carpet that is her life. There is more, though, than the truth that we are each responsible for every thought, every feeling, every action that makes up the dream that is the life that each of us lives, and that is that the miraculous is available to every one of us at every moment, and that the extent of it far surpasses anything we can ordinarily imagine.

What Philippa has been given to see, hear, taste, touch and know is that the realm of the extraordinary is to be found at every moment amidst the ordinary and mundane, and that there, in the middle of the routine and the humdrum of daily life, lies angelic help, eternally present, awaiting only upon our own invitation to be able to manifest in all its splendour and in everything that transpires. That is the reality she strives now to teach, to communicate and to give to all those who are ready to learn. The journey is never ending, and it is not without its inescapable tribulations, pains and sufferings. This book marks the first in the series that will document the evolution of the teaching that is hers to bring to humanity in its hour of need.

Pippa and I found our lives interwoven thanks to an introduction from Don, another remarkable character whose own journey is as fantastical as is his telling of his tales. Don is another larger than life phenomenon whose journey through life threatening illness forced him to uncover the fact that life has meaning and that this alone would enable him to move forward into a new life. Philippa was part of that early renaissance in his life. It was his gift in our shared search for the healing of the Perthe's Disease of one of my sons to introduce us. I was engaged in the same dedicated and committed way that Pippa was searching to make whole her traumatised and profoundly wounded daughter, both of us refusing to believe the standard conclusions that a full return to normal life would be impossible. This refusal to give up in the search for what could only be called the miraculous, forms part of what is so movingly told in the pages of this book.

When Pippa and I met, our first conversation invoked an

immediacy of relationship and understanding - the sort that normally comes to grace a relationship only after years of friendship, and it happened even though the exchange took place on the telephone. So alive was that conversation that I knew we had to meet immediately, but I could not move at the time so the first meeting in person occurred in Oxford between Pippa and my wife. Rapidly thereafter Pippa came to give healing to our son – a visit that we planned for one afternoon but which resulted in our spending a few days together in our accommodation in a medieval moated manor in Hereford. What is so striking about my memories of those first meetings is that despite the seriousness of our mission, we nevertheless played and laughed with an unusual lightness of being! I have indelible images of her colour cards coming out, spread out across the expanse of the floor or on the kitchen table, being played with by the children, under the gaze of her eager, piercing dark eyes, gleaming out from under a shock of hair, her seeming frailty belieing the extraordinary strength and integrity of her energy and above all her Will.

Rescued by Angels is an epic tale of awakening through the suffering of a life genuinely lived. It is the awakening to ever evolving and deepening meaning and to the reality of the simultaneous existence of the multiple dimensions co-existing at every moment in all of our lives. It is told simply, precisely, and directly – no frills. It was written in a matter of a few weeks in response to an inner imperative and following the instruction of the angelic beings who had come to participate in her life, so that you might read it just the way it is. Through innocence and naivety, breakdown and breakthrough, Pippa's story takes us through the devastating earlier years of her life, sharing with us her instruction and education starting with the realms of colour, on into the laws of harmony and revelation. In the pages of this book you will read the true story of miracle after miracle foretold and realised – step by step, episode by episode, from unknown to unknown, calling each one of us ever deeper in our journey of obedience and evolution.

I feel blessed to have been asked to write this foreword and I do so in the hope that if there is any doubt in you about whether to buy the book or proceed on, I might implore you and inspire you to do so. I write as a conventionally trained physician, a medical homoeopath, a healer, scientist, editor, artist, father, husband, friend. In all my years of practice and research it is the work that Pippa and I and a small group of healers on five continents have engaged in over nearly 5 years that has most challenged and inspired me. Through the inspiration and leadership of Suzanne Mendelssohn, our obedience healer in America, we have come to know at ever deeper levels the fabric of some of the energetic realms, and we know that this must now be communicated as much and as extensively as possible. In Pippa's life, part of this manifestation is what she calls Metatronic Healing, an entire system of energetic transformation that she has been given to teach and develop. It is my fervent hope that you will go on to read this story and be inspired to listen to the whisperings in your own life and so to open to the angelic presences that await only your invitation to begin manifesting their miracles daily in your life.

As Pippa's story makes abundantly clear, there is no short cut, no panacea that will obviate the friction required to bring about the awakening. What it also demonstrates beyond any doubt, is that if we remain faithful to our conscience, true to our principles, and fervently in pursuit of surrender and service to our fellow beings, we will always be responded to and always rewarded. The price is obedience to a higher order *no matter what the cost*. Pippa is paying that price as we journey on. This book is part of that fee. Read it, enjoy it and know that in the honesty of this one human being's surrender lie the seeds of your own salvation. Perhaps these closing words of Eliot's will serve to end as they served to begin:

"We shall not cease from exploration
And the end of all our exploring
Will be to arrive where we started
And know the place for the first time."
T.S. Eliot   Little Gidding

Dr. Kim A Jobst MA. DM. MRCP. MFHom
Hereford. 2008

The Miracle

Hello, and it's good to meet you – whoever you are. Let me introduce myself. I'm a healer of sorts. No, I must modify that: none of us are healers – not of other people, anyway. But we are all healers of ourselves.

We come here, to this long-suffering planet, to heal, to become whole, to open our hearts, to learn to love; and this means that on our journeys we experience the very opposite of all of these.

No, we don't heal other people, in fact that's the mistake most of us make in trying to do life at all. We try to fix him, or her, or them, in the hope that this will make things rather more comfortable for *us*, and we fail to take the good look at ourselves which would actually save us a lot of time and hassle.

But when we are ready for a little healing, a little whole-ing (which is really all that the word 'healing' means), that is when we can turn to one another and ask for some help. "No man is an island" – that old Italian poet was right. We're all part of one another; we're quantum soup. Even our thoughts radically affect what's happening out there, in the world, with all the other people as well as ourselves.

So none of us are healers and all of us are healers: we each hold a space for another person – lots of people, in fact, and they each hold a space for us.

Healing implies returning to oneness, and because ultimately we are all one, the division and separation that we often feel are nothing more than an illusion. We stand beside one another; we each let another one know that they are not alone; we remind them in some way of who they truly are. We stand united, so that our friend, our loved one, our client, can reconnect with the wholeness that they never really left behind, but only mislaid or forgot about for a while.

Nearly fifteen years ago, my child, my beautiful, blonde-

1

haired, gentle-natured, six-year-old daughter, was hit by a car. The doctors held out no hope for her at all. They operated on her brain twice in the first 36 hours; they put everything they had into saving her life.

She 'died' twice; and when she then lived, they made it perfectly clear that they didn't understand it at all. What about the brain damage? This had already happened, they said. The outlook was about as grim as it could be. And then she came out of her coma and smiled.

Less than four weeks later, she took 50 tottering steps down the hospital corridor before being wheeled to the car that was waiting to take her home.

Today, she is a vibrant young adult – bright and shining. Her journey back to wholeness has been long and arduous; it's taken all the courage she could find. But there she is, at university, reading Early Childhood Studies.

She has vast ambitions: she will create orphanages, she says, to take children out of the shocking slavery into which they have been so disgracefully sold. She walks, she runs, she laughs.

How did this happen? We don't entirely know, not for certain. The world is full of wonders and mysteries – and mysteries, by their very nature, cannot be reasoned. We know that what occurred was a miracle: in other words, it cannot be explained or measured by any of our conventional tools.

This close encounter with her death was the worst, but not the only, event in a chapter of what we generally tend to call disasters, which befell my family and me throughout the 1990s. But it was precisely that chapter of accidents, and above all the long search for the miracles of healing that would restore my child to full health, which led eventually to the birth of a healing system at once ancient and contemporary: it was a gift from spirit, which rapidly showed itself to be vital, radical and profound in its effects.

Nothing happens overnight: all significant or useful discoveries tend to come at the end of a journey of some kind. This book recounts parts of my journey because – like all journeys – these had a purpose: they pushed me into a place where surrender to an authority way beyond my own was the only powerful choice. Healing revelations, or any revelations, come to that, tend to arrive at the moments when ego has collapsed; it has given up its usual reliance on its own resources, generally because it has tried repeatedly to do life single-handed, and failed.

In essence, this narrative is one of survival against very high odds: it is a roller-coaster of disasters that nearly crushed us, not once but several times, and divine rescue that came over and over again to our aid. I'm offering it to you here as an "if-you-can-survive-this-you-can-handle-anything!" kind of promise, in the knowledge that when we hand over to the powers of the Universe, which are so much greater than we are, they respond to us every time, with love in action.

If you are looking for healing, for a better quality of life, for more self-belief or harmony or prosperity or health or joy or faith, you will find something in here that will help you.

Hindsight is a wonderful thing: look back with the 20:20 lenses that come with the passing of time and you see life as more of a game, or a practice in role play, than it ever seemed while you were living it. It's a scene, or an ongoing series of scenes, set up by us and for us, so that we find our dormant skills and polish them up.

Shakespeare told us that the world's a stage and all of us are players, and of course he was right. In the context of our own lives, our own 'stages', we try on various costumes; we do different roles, according to the time and place. In the end, it's all a question of choice: we can do comedy, we can do tragedy; which do we go for?

So just to reassure you that – like all stories – this one finally has a happy ending, and also to remind you that the only thing that is real is now, we will start the journey with something which, in this particular tale, pretty much represents the present day.

The present, after all, is the gift; it's the miracle of life itself, in each moment that we are living it.

Before we set off for the frozen Northern counties of England, where much of my little family drama was set, let's take a trip to sunnier climes because, as T.S. Eliot said "to make an end is to make a beginning. The end is where we start from." This makes the greatest sense, because the moment when we reach the end of our tethers is most often the starting point, the place where our lives have a real chance of opening up to miracles.

I'd suggest you make yourself a nice cup of tea, then, and take a short trip with me to sunny California – or to some place of your own where you, too, feel that the Universe is thoroughly benevolent and kind. Put your feet up, take a few deep breaths (always a good idea) and enjoy the story.

One

Reality is what happens
when you take out the insulation

1

March 2008

There's no music like the roar of this great ocean as the surf crashes back and forth, pulsing out its beat on the faces of the rocks. There's no place on earth that more extravagantly paints the heart of nature: her shocking optimism, her reckless bounty.

"There's plenty more where that came from."

This is her message, bold and lucid, like the bright sky above. Baby-blue, still as the Buddha, the sky is a perfect meditation.

A deep bark resonates across the water; it's the call of a lone seal, lodged on a distant pier as a fishing boat imports its haul. She's answered by the one I'm watching, a male, glorious in his clumsy obesity, rising to full height on a flat rock nearby. His harem and families mostly doze around him; from time to time a youngster will belly-flop its way to the rock-edge and slither into the foam. Farther off, a sea-otter lies face-up, paws crossed like a kitten. He basks a while, checks out his neighbours, then shoots back down to the rich kelp below. A flock of pelicans flies overhead in perfect V-formation. Are they out to fish or just having fun?

The mountainous landscape behind us is young and bold, untamed. The ocean is surely the wildest on the planet, yet they call it the Pacific – a sea of peace.

I breathe luxuriously, filling my lungs with air so clean I almost feel it squeak: there's nothing between me and a few small islands dotted far, far south; nothing but animals, vegetables, a vast expanse of water and endless sky.

All around the weathered bench on which we sit, the succulents are in bloom: sun-filled petals in bright, rainbow hues. Their juicy leaves look good enough to eat.

I feel blue. No, not doldrums-blue. Madonna-blue. Peaceful-blue. In-love-with-all-the-world-blue.

"You would do," my new friend Carina remarks, "with the aphrodisiacs you just swallowed – all those prawns and figs."

No, really. It's deeper than that. More substantial. I love my fellow man and woman – most of them anyway. I just wound up a workshop on the English coast and I'm filling my tanks on the Californian coast – my favourite spot in all the world, the one that I call home. It's a place that could stop your heart – or start it.

The workshop was vital and turbulent and ultimately peaceful, like the sea. My job is not a job; it's a forum to chat about the most fascinating stuff on earth. There's another peace-ticket.

"What kind of workshop?" asks Carina. Like I said, she's a *new* friend.

"Archangels," I reply.

A raising of the eyebrows, ever so slight.

"The most fascinating stuff on *earth*?"

"Uh-huh," I nod.

"Doing what?"

"Tuning people into their energy, to work with them. They're really quite pro-active."

"Is that like Reiki or something?"

"Yes but not really."

But more of that later. I like Carina. I don't want to frighten her off when we only just met; nor you, dear reader, come to that. But you get the picture: it's all love and bright lights; angels walk among us; heaven and earth are one. The poets said it better: "God's in his heaven and all's right with the world."

Not three yards from where we sit, a pair of Canada geese flutter and sway in their graceful courtship dance. It's obviously a set-up, to prove my point.

An old thought arrives in my head, one that many of us have heard before:

"Most men lead lives of quiet desperation."

"And that means women too, I suppose?" I reply, a little

sharply. "No, Mr Thoreau, you got it wrong." Quite wrong.

Life is a cabaret, a positive jamboree: come on and join the dance! This wonderful world is a firework show, all divine sparks and shooting stars, each one aglow with pure potential. They're for us and with us and in us, there for the taking. We're kings, queens, artists all. How could we possibly be quiet, or desperate?

Or have I forgotten a thing or two? Maybe I'd best back up, to one of the places where the story began. We can choose any moment we please, of course, if we're looking to the past for clues, but some are more obvious than others. I think I'll opt for the simple phone call – the one that changed it all.

2

August 1990

I'm about to leave a marriage that's been a bad dream, but I don't know it yet. I don't really know even that I'm in the bad dream, or that the dream is about to up its pace and scale. I'm Dorothy Gale in 'Kansas City', only half-awake; my world is monochromatic and dim. I know that something's wrong but I can't see too clearly. That's the thing about a grey world: nothing is clearly defined.

It's good where we live. We've grown a lovely home in a town with a thriving university; good schools, wholesome families, music, theatre, parks. It's a middle-class ghetto, perhaps, but safe. And right now it's early evening; light is streaming through the windows both ends of the beautiful kitchen-dining room we've made in the basement. The children are usefully employed, cleaning out their gerbils, building spaceships. I'm cradling the little one in one arm, peeling carrots with the other. Best friends around the corner, up the road; tennis on Tuesday; piano on Wednesday; a party next week.

This is not the stuff of deep reflection. The comfortable routine is a good cushion; it gives distraction from the inner rumblings of tumult. I'm a good Catholic girl, or slightly good: I follow the rules. You've made your bed, they say, you lie on it. Having a tricky time on earth? Hey well guess what – it's all good in heaven; store up your brownie points and use them later. Which seems to suggest that dead is good: stay in the grey zone if you want to survive. So I do what I'm told: I positively *die*, for years on end. And then comes the phone call.

It's simple enough, a job offer for my husband. There have been a few of those already. He's out of work and I'm busy with these three youngsters, so we rather depend on his being employed. This new offer, though, is beyond the pale; I nearly forget to pass the message on. But he's back from his soldierly escapades – the business that occupies him most weekends – and I tell him anyway.

"You'll never guess what they're offering you now."

The opportunity he is being offered comes from the frozen North, miles from anywhere you'd want to be in a million years, and it's utterly preposterous; the job is in a smallish town where everything is built of dark depressing northern stuff. We don't *do* dark, cold, depressing; we do warm, light, golden stone: sunny side up. The whole idea is obviously nothing more than a joke, he's surely not going to take it seriously? Oh blow me down, I do believe he is. If this man decides that destination deep freeze is where his family is headed, you're made of sterner stuff than I am if you dare to resist.

So I'm in there already, down the road to the future, led there by default, and I'm listening to this unlikely proposal. If it had come as a written invitation from the hobgoblins (they're well-known for their mischief) it would have run something like this:

"Come up North to where the grass is greener."

"Leave behind your comfortable home," it would have continued, "and take on some adventure, show your mettle. True, you may miss your suburban comforts, your friends and schools and shops. With the bills you're paying, though, do you have a lot of choice? Think of the small fortune you'll stash in the bank when you sell your lovely home. You've worked for it, you've earned it. We invite you to live in an old farmhouse: ponies and dogs for the children; land for the husband, stress-free."

Stress-free is good. I can't argue with that.

"But it's straw-in-your-ears up there," I interrupt. "Isn't it? Mud flats; deep and meaningful chats around the price of corn."

(*I'm more of a city girl myself.*)

"What *is* this place anyway? There's no theatre, no concert-hall; no *university*. Ridiculous."

"True," they admit. "Not too many people to chat with, maybe, but what's that when those daily anxieties fall off your shoulders? You'll be living the rural idyll. Embrace the challenge!"

The course has already been set, of course; it was decided the moment I passed the message on. Nevertheless, I must make some mental arrangements with myself. I must convince myself, for one thing, that there is good reason why we must take this crazy action, and I must persuade myself that I'm being pro-active in this business of the life decisions that will impact so deeply on the futures of us all. Well that's down to money, and it's been three months now without a pay-cheque: they're close to the bone when they claim there's not a lot of choice.

For another thing, I must reason myself into believing that the crazy action will bring clear benefits. That's down to the parenting factor: a farm has been my husband's longest-standing fantasy – he's been talking about it for years – and a happy parent cherishes his children, right? Not that he'd have time to do any serious farming, of course; just enough to be peaceful. All that harmony with nature; all that quality time enjoying life with his kids...

The hobgoblins will spend the next few days and weeks wriggling their way into my ears, my eyes, my heart. I will push down the foreboding in my gut and bury it deep. Maybe, I will tell myself, just maybe, if he gets his dream...

A few weeks later and we're down in that lovely kitchen of ours again, the heart of our home. There's a bang as the front door is opened and slammed, a crash as keys are thrown down and boots kicked off. That hiking last weekend has let off less steam than I'd hoped. He's home and he's headed in our direction down the stairs.

I'm holding the little one just a fraction tighter, tucking her into that space close to my ribs. The others head for a hole behind the sofa: their safe space.

3

Excellent move

"Excellent move," says the estate agent, rubbing his hands. "A gem of a house, if I may say so. It'll be gone in a week."

"Excellent move," say the money-lenders. "A full bridging loan? Of course; no problem. No problem at all."

This is the potted version. It is how, in the space of a few short months, we leave behind home, family, friends, schools, all modern conveniences and central heating – everything, in fact, that renders us relatively secure and safe – and find ourselves camping in a derelict farmhouse with a well that's run dry and no mains water, separated from the nearest neighbour by fields on all sides, the whole lot covered in snow.

I'm married to a man who should have been a paratrooper. He's Mr Outward Bound. His idea of recreation is a trek through mud and snow, a survival course in a damp forest, rubbing sticks and frying worms. Never felt the cold in his life. He *likes* it here.

I'm a city girl – oh, but I said that already. Still, to flesh out the picture, my idea of recreation is a gentle stroll in Hyde Park on a sunny afternoon, coffee in Starbucks, a seat in the Stalls (any stage will do; West End's good); a theme park with the kids; shopping in Rome.

"Dream on," say the hobgoblins. "You've never even been to Rome."

"OK, I'll dream on; I'm good at that. What is a life without dreams?"

Oh, and I rely on outer sources of heat – I wear sweaters in August.

Funny that it's me then, right here, that I'm the one trudging across the ice-hard fields, buckets in hand, fetching water from the tap at the end of the field, while Mr Outward Bound sits in a centrally heated office, reached each day by company car, with not-so-occasional commutes to warmer climes down South.

A line goes through my head; I've read it somewhere – it probably comes from a Buddhist teacher:

"Before enlightenment, chop wood carry water. After enlightenment, chop wood carry water."

(Mr Outward Bound chops wood – I'll give him that.)

But I can't imagine what the line means. And there's not a lot of time for reflection. I have a twelve-year-old daughter and a nine-year-old son suffering culture shock and any other kind of shock that has a name. Like young seedlings in spring, they have been uprooted from all that they know, and they've been planted out not in a friendly fertile space but in ground that's frozen, barren, and unsympathetic in every conceivable way.

The eldest child is containing her grief in the privacy of her bedroom, scant endorphins provided courtesy of Michael Jackson, her only and vital antidote to deep trauma. The middle one is more direct; his wrath is expressed moment by moment, in your face, full-on: fists, feet, lungs – anything will do.

The little one, the three-year-old, has been watching it all in silence. She's too stunned to speak. She can sing, though. At three going on four, she has nearly perfect pitch. They've picked her out at nursery school to start the carol service with a solo: "Oh little Star of Bethlehem," she'll be chanting, "How still we see thee rise." I hear her in the mornings, practising from the safety of her bed: "While mortals sleep the angels keep their watch of wondering love."

I don't believe a word of it but it's a comfort all the same.

The builders arrived a week after we did and set to work on the roof. That means the old thatching has gone: it was tucked nice and snug beneath the tiles, the first cushion against the icy gales, but they said it was a fire hazard so it went. The old plaster's gone too, revealing bricks that are none too clean and tidy. This absence of plaster and insulation leaves an open space of eight inches or so where the walls would usually meet the roofing beams and felt, which makes for easy access by the winds that shriek and roar their way down the nearby hills, careering like howling wolves towards every open space and crack. The horizontal blizzards bring snow – fresh supplies daily – straight into the upstairs rooms.

These constant supplies of frozen water on the upper landing are about it, on the freshwater front. There's a sink in the room that passes for a kitchen, so water will flow out even if there's none coming in – excuse the heavy symbolism. There's no cooking stove, of course; never mind, we brought the microwave from the old house. It would be superfluous to complain about the absence of a fridge because the winter that kicked in a month ago, just a few weeks after we arrived, is the coldest one on record. So the scene is set: we're camping in the snow, and it's getting thicker by the day.

It's 9.15 in the morning. I've taken the kids to school, got the water in. I'm wearing hat and scarf, boots and gloves. The inside temperature reads minus 13 degrees centigrade. I'm staring at an open grate in the downstairs room, the single source of heat for the seven rooms of this Georgian gem. A nice cup of coffee with a friend would be good but I don't know anyone around here so there's nowhere to go. My brain seems to be slowing down; it's getting quite fuzzy. I think to myself:

"I need sticks, kindling."

That means a hike through a blizzard to an outhouse near the stables and I'm numb, fossilised, way past shivering, so going out again doesn't feel like an option just at present. What to do? How to pass the day?

The shaking was quite violent a moment or two ago but I don't have to worry, it seems to be calming itself. A moment later I lose consciousness; I'm on the floor, out cold in more ways than one.

It kills you, doesn't it, hypothermia? It's an easy death, no big deal – Mr Outward Bound told me all about it. You get beyond the pain, the bone-chewing exposure that slashes your cheeks and eats up your fingers and toes, and fall into a quiet coma, as you drift away to a peaceful place and never wake again.

So who woke me? There's no-one around; no brandy and blankets or rubs and the temperature still way down in the deep freeze. But it's five hours later and I'm awake. I'm rubbing my hands and my feet. It's a chilly place I've landed, that's for sure: but what's new?

The unexamined life is not worth living? Well, Mr Socrates, there's no time for reflection or metaphors on the cold life. Action is the only thing that will keep this show on the road. It's half past two: I'm off for the school round.

4

A word of advice

Don't buy one house before you've sold the first one – not if you're doing it on borrowed money.

Let's review the game plan, rewind the reel to where we were soon after the invitation arrived. The plot went like this: The sale of our Oxford house will pay off the mortgage and set free a comfortable capital lump. This will cover the purchase price of the new place and all the renovations. Net result? No mortgage loan; and money in the bank.

Throw in a pony or two, cats and dogs, fresh farm produce (organic of course), a tractor – maybe a goat. The Good Life: it looks quite reasonable on paper. And you never know, perhaps it'll even be fun.

Two of the elements necessary for survival – water and fire – are in pretty short supply, around these parts. Ah, but the lack of those is more than met by the abundance of the other ones: no shortage of earth, for instance; there's acres and acres of the stuff. There's air too, up here in the hills. The wind is one of the special effects on this little estate; it stays on duty around the clock, 365 days a year. When the Northerly gales take a break, they hand over to the ones from the East. The previous owners introduced some quaint touches of their own: they knocked down half the house, leaving an inside wall – matchbox thick – to do battle with those fierce North-Eastern elements – or the lack of them.

"To save on heating bills," they explained.

"Heating?" – I buttoned my lip.

We've got the curtains, though, the prettiest things you ever saw, run up by interior designers and paid for by the company in the "soft furnishings allowance". They've got pelmets, sashes: the bright colours of their glorious fabrics hang, ludicrous against the backdrop of decayed plaster and wreckage, like gaudy paper over a parcel of rubble. They were intended to be the finishing touches on our Georgian gem, not stage props for a farce.

We've revived the name the house was given when it was built by its 1780s owners. Salmonby Grange: a graceful name, for the age of elegance when it was built – all Jane Austen and chamber-maids, carriages and pianos and ballroom dance. It suggests the elegant home of a landed gentleman, fishing peacefully on a sunny Sunday afternoon. Stress-free.

Nicola's been seeing odd lights moving in her walls at night: there's nothing peaceful about those; they come with whines and whispers and send shivers down her spine. This house has none of the grace and favour of a Georgian age: no Sunday afternoons, no peaceful waters; how could there possibly be salmon? The place reeks of a darker, more complex time, of secret griefs and hidden rage. In the privacy of my head, it has a different name completely. I've called it Wuthering Heights.

But we've got the horses, and the dog too. This is the first thing I have done; my OTT response to guilt. OK kids, you've left everyone you love and all you know and landed in Siberia: let's go for a pony ride, let's walk the dog!

All of that happened in record time, late last year, and now we're well into February. We've had our house, our beloved home in Oxford, up for sale since September, just before we secured the deeds for the farm, and just before the housing market dived and crashed.

I'm in Oxford because my friend Jamie has called – for the third time: "It's the squatters," he says. "Sorry to be the messenger again – it looks worse this time."

It goes like this: you rent the house out while it's up *For Sale*, a hopeful buyer shows up, the tenants flee and overnight, the squatters arrive. They smash a window or a door and settle in. I'm here to clean up the piles of crumpled newspapers, the upturned cartons of rancid milk, the floor that's turned into a public latrine.

17

Turning out squatters is not a job for Paratroopers and Outward Bounders, it seems; it's a 340-mile round trip and "highly inconvenient." No, it's over to me, and whatever allies and repairs men I can find.

The children are here though – they won't let me do it alone. They're the greatest allies a girl could wish for; they're Dorothy's three best friends, the ones she found on Planet Oz.

We bed down in sleeping bags for the night, Wispa the dog right beside us all. Darkness descends and the tramps try to force another entry but she sends them running – she'd wake the whole street with the noise she makes. What a good thing they don't know that beneath the bark is a heart as soft as butter.

There's something else, far more inconvenient than the squalor that we're here to fix. We're six months down the line now, and funds are running drier than the Salmonby well. There's more money going out to the usurers each month than I've ever seen in my life, all borrowed – of course – against the value of this unsold place, the house I'm standing in right now.

I'm in the kitchen-dining room, the heart of our old home, but it doesn't belong to us any more. On paper we are still the owners; in reality it belongs to the men at the bank. The inheritance I've been given over the years by the small stream of deceased loved ones, all of which I've put into the building of my children's home, it's going, going, gone – we're nearly at the last cent.

But here we are; the dear old house is all clean again and I'm remembering a thing my friend Alison said a few years back as we stood together in this same spot, all Laura Ashley and Italian tiles: "Everyone should lose everything at least once in a lifetime. I've done it twice. It was very good for me both times."

Alison is older than me, and mysterious: a kind of wise woman, who swoops into a life when she's needed and vanishes just as fast. She's befriended me while my mother is dying – God knows I need it. But she says the strangest things.

"That was a random remark," I think to myself as I ask her the details.

I've logged it all the same, and I recall it now, as I pack up the children and dogs and head back up North. Losing everything you have and crash-landing in Siberia, *good* for you?

"Time, ladies and gentlemen, it's time."

5

On making plans

The hobgoblins must have been having a field day. There were three things, they told me, that we'd get for the price of our move: the first two of those were (i) no money worries and (ii) a great family life. So here's the score:

i) we are on the fast lane to bankruptcy and the road back home is closed;
ii) family life is right there on the same track.

I'm standing in that other kitchen now, back at the farm. The builders turned tail last month; they disappeared into thin air. They work for money, of course; why would they hang around now? They've replaced the old roof, but not a lot else, it appears. The gaping holes are still wide open and it all seems much the same: diseased windows, crumbling walls.

So the hobgoblins were wrong on the first two suggestions. What was the third thing they promised? Oh that was it: the city girl and the farmers; no-one to talk to. Maybe they've stood by that one, just for fun. Kick the city girl into shape, push her off her high haunches into the real world, all alone.

So maybe this is it; perhaps this is where we get to stay, for the rest of time. We're in hell and it's frozen over. And hell is a walled place, a dank prison where you do solitary confinement, hanging out with memories and corpses; you don't get to chat.

There's an odd thing happening in this village, in the place that was once a stronghold of the local church. It's an international teaching place of some kind and it happens in the Old Manor. Maybe there's a new religion growing up inside its walls. Maybe something has come in to give the old place a breath of fresh air and wake the village up. I've heard that some of the local workers stop their tractor tracks in springtime, startled by the women fluttering arms and hands, their colourful robes swaying in the breeze.

We're invited to visit and take a look around – yes, Mr Outward Bound too. Well, why not? There's precious little to do around here otherwise. So we've accepted, and here we are at the front door. We're greeted by a smiling face we've never met before, the original Glinda, the benevolent Witch of Planet Oz, blonde curls flowing. The name by which she likes to be called, though, is Sunflower.

"Welcome," she says, beaming her Good-Witch glow right through us. "How *are* you?"

"Oh, er – good, thanks. We're good."

"That's good," she says, gazing into our eyes. "That's really good. I'm really happy to hear that."

"Oh, er – good."

The beatific smile continues, the eye contact unwavering – not a flicker. Mr Outward Bound generally has a beam of his own. He can outstare anyone with an expression that would freeze the summer roses, but here even he is faintly unnerved.

"Thanks for giving us your time," I continue, shuffling my feet.

"You're so welcome."

We move on at last, as we follow Sunflower to a beautiful garden, a pond, a fountain. There's a dining hall where a group of students is chatting, tea in hands. They're all brightly clad, a positive rainbow. Each room has a colour theme; they're decked out in violets or pinks, indigos or brightest yellow. There are pictures on every wall, meditations in green, turquoise, gold.

Most surprising are the small glass bottles: what on earth are these? They are neatly arranged in luminous shelves, whole sets of them all over the place, each containing brightly coloured fluids, sparkling like gems.

It's warm. Central heating warm.

I peel off a sweater and blink a few times. We've never seen a place like this in our lives. We must have landed on Oz for real; that explains it all. There was a cyclone; our home took flight; everything was grey and confused. And then we walked through a door right into an alternative reality. There's a problem, though: where did the door go? It's disappeared, along with the grey world behind it. That ticket we bought to the new reality was one-way only. Bad decision.

The students are still chatting. I overhear talk of auras, rebirthing, ascended masters, whatever they may be. There are earnest interchanges around the notions of spirit guides, astrology charts, energy. I could sure do with some of that; mine's been running thin for a while now.

"I met my soul mate last month," one woman is saying, "I just know it. We're really connected? We've spent the last five lifetimes together, maybe more. He gets it; he totally gets it, all of it."

"All of what?" OK, don't ask.

"You're so lucky," replies her friend. "I'm alone right now, but I had this wonderful reading with Enoch the other day. My twin flame's coming in next year. Isn't that great!"

"Enoch's wonderful," replies her friend. "He sees all the really useful stuff. He says my spirit guide is an antelope – how cool is that?"

"That mandala this morning, wasn't it *amazing*?" says the first woman. "Did you *feel* the energy?"

"Mock all you please, girl; resist all you like," say the hobgoblins. "You made your bed; you lie in it, remember."

"You could have warned me," I'm thinking.

Our new friend is taking us over for introductions. The woman in deep magenta has not spoken yet. She's been gazing at me in the most disconcerting way. She gets up from the table and takes hold of my hand:

"It's so beautiful that you've felt drawn to visit – I'm glad," she says. Her name is Parvati.

"Really glad," she continues. "I feel I know you; I can see the light behind you."

"I beg your pardon?"

I glance around, check out the bulbs: no lights. She smiles benignly.

"I feel we're meant to spend time together," she says. "Would you like a reading?"

A what? It's another planet; that's for sure. I'll be needing a phrase book. No I won't. I won't *be* here; how could I possibly hang around in a universe as alien as this? A voice inside me has been crying out its frantic request since the moment we touched down on this planet last year, ever since that door behind us vanished into thin air.

"I want to go home. I want to go home."

Right here, right now, in this place with its central heating and kindly people, the voice is reaching screaming pitch. I want to turn around and run right out of the front gate; and I want to keep on running, all the way back to Oxford. But I'm far too polite; and I've nowhere to go.

"Make fun or make misery," continues the inner nudge, friendlier now. "You'll get friendship here, and conversation; maybe more. There are seers and prophets right nearby."

It's a voice from the future. But my ears are deaf. Or nearly, perhaps not quite, because I feel a murmur, an inner whisper:

"Maybe," says the faint stirring, "just maybe, there's a wizard hereabouts. Maybe he will help you. You said you're looking for your way back home – remember?"

"There's an in-house supper at the weekend," says my new acquaintance with the flowing magenta velvet. "Come and join us, do."

Does something in my face convey a whisper of hope, a hint of warmth on the horizon? Because my husband is escorting me firmly back to the car, his expression more thunderous even than usual. And now, in a silence that would deafen the BFG, he is driving me back to Wuthering Heights.

It's nearly Christmas.

6

Spring 1991

"It makes you laugh with delight that anything so fantastic could exist on this sombre earth."

This is how Somerset Maugham wrote of Siam in 1925. He was staying at the Oriental Hotel in Bangkok, as Rudyard Kipling and Joseph Conrad had done before him. It's not surprising; the rich fertility of this country is any writer's dream. In 1939 the country took on a new name: it became Thailand, which means Land of the Free.

Think of gleaming deep-brown bodies, their faces grinning from ear to ear, as they squat at the base of their house-ladders, washing and bathing in the river below. Think of elephants and crocodiles, and of a natural amphitheatre as big as France; of water drenching the hillsides in exuberant vegetation. Think of roses and orchids, butterflies and exotic blossoms in every hue. Think of everything that isn't Siberia, the frozen North, Wuthering Heights. Water flushes the flowers and carries their powerful perfumes into the air; it nurtures wild fruits; it provides a habitat for rice paddies and for fish, a staple protein in this tropical paradise.

"If you really want to understand us," a former Thai Prime Minister has advised, "you must understand water. We are a water people, fluid, but unbreakable."

Ah yes, now *that* I understand – even from our own little parched zone back in the frozen North.

The original heart of this land, the city of Ayutthaya, could only be reached by river; the boats billowed up to this enchanted city on the monsoon wind.

Early explorers were spellbound by what they saw: a place that looked as though it were made of gold. Well it was, more or less: the wats, the Buddhist temple-monasteries, set the place aglow – all 1700 of them - with gilded spires and altars heaped with that glorious gleaming metal.

All this treasure, of course, would not withstand the pressure of human greed. Ayutthaya was seized by the Burmese in 1767, its wats destroyed, its gold melted, its entire heritage looted and razed to the ground.

The resilient Thai people reclaimed their land but would not disturb their shattered gods. So another city was built later in a site downstream. The king called it the City of Angels, Abode of the Emerald Buddha. It's known to the rest of us as Bangkok.

I'm here with my son. He and I need all we can get of all of the things the Minister has suggested: freedom, water, faith, resilience, the fantastic, exuberant joy; the encouragement to rebuild our lives in a new and unfamiliar place.

The warmth here goes without saying: the sun blasts down on this lush tropical landscape every day of the year. I'm in the business of child rescue – my own children, that is. It's not only the physical thermostat that's been in need of repair at Wuthering Heights; the emotional one is lethal – there's the real hypothermia. The Far East solution will fix both of these for a while as our bodies swelter and our hearts are set on fire. Granted, it's a temporary remedy, but something's got to be better than nothing.

We're so hot, in fact, that I can barely stand upright, but we don't have to. The tuk-tuk darts between the cars and buses as we bounce up and down like footballs on our well-worn seats. The grand central streets burst with glossy and exotic shops but we're headed down the back streets, our eyes on stalks as we see the naked bodies scampering up and down stick-ladders in dwellings cobbled together from rough planks and cardboard boxes. Only yards around the corner are the Westerners luxuriating by their hotel pools, just as we were half an hour ago.

Maybe we're not quite broke after all: not now, not this minute, not beside all of this. In my heart I know that it's *my* money I've used for this trip, funds inherited years ago but vanished year on year in the whirlwind of a paratrooper's rage.

How this has happened is not important here; it matters only that the absence of funds has been a key symptom in a marriage that's long since been headed for the rocks. So I'm reclaiming a little joy on behalf of my child; I'm borrowing against a future that was bankrupted long ago, and I'm glad. Just for today, my boy is living a life that is joyful and warm. There's wonderment radiating from his every pore.

We're exploring this crazy bustling city as I look for wooden ducks. I've started a business, you see. Maybe it's not just Stephen I'm rescuing. I suspect I may have started on the business of rescuing myself, reclaiming my own, Eastern dimension, as it were – stimulating some kind of inner yin. I'm setting up in a small way as an import agent. It's a wonderful alibi for a few short weeks of fun with a boy who's a superstar, my hero of heroes.

We find fishes and elephants, boxes and doorstops, candlesticks and bunches of flowers, made of softwood and colourwashed in gentle tones. They are beautiful and they've not yet flooded every gift shop in the West.

This is a good start, but the silks! Wound up on boards and lined like books along an everlasting set of shelves, they glitter and glow like polished gems: turquoise and crimson, sapphire and rose; every possible tint and tone, from peach to ochre, deep forest green to pale lime, royal purple to spring lilac. I want it – all of it. And what would I do with it if I had it? I'd feast my eyes on it, every day. I would drink in the colours and bask in their glowing light.

We take a different return route, the tourist path this time, as our driver takes us past grand palaces and glowing temples. He's proud of his heritage and our faces are reward enough: we're struck dumb.

As we enter one of the temples and amble slowly in the shade, there's an awesome stillness that removes us completely from the bustling noise outside. There are no chairs in this place, but mats on the floor invite us to sit a while, to bathe quietly in the tranquillity of the golden Buddhas and silent gongs.

I feel a slight movement inside me; some darkened inner room is opening its rusty door, making way for a glimmer of something unfamiliar. I'd dare to call it a hint of light and hope, a whisper of peace.

But there's more to see and savour: we've scarcely begun. Temple or palace, there are whole walls of lapis lazuli, others of gold; emeralds and rubies everywhere.

Every hue, tint or tone the universe has ever dreamed up is here in this chaotic city and throughout the land, twinkling, sparkling, dazzling my eyes and cells. I was raised in post-World War II Britain – a colourless landscape if ever there was one. These startling hues feel like a wake-up call: why have I never felt this before, the sheer energy and power that comes at you in these stunning, multi-coloured rays of sun?

"Dorothy, you're not in Kansas any more."

It's time for supper. Thai food is my new discovery, my novel delight. This is long before a chain of Thai Orchids springs up in all the back-streets of England, offering chicken curry and coconut desserts. It's a novelty for Stephen too, this curry and Eastern spice, but he'll pass on that, thanks. The hotel can do better than ginger and chillies in this small boy's paradise: he gets hamburger and chips every day for three weeks.

We visit the Rose Garden, the Floating Market, the Crocodile Farm. We travel deep into the jungle, where elephants shamble on silent, rubbery feet down a path to the river, with only the faint clinking of their polished chains and the hollow ring of their teakwood bells to break the silence. The Mahout offer Stephen a friendly hand as he clambers up the ear of a willing matriarch.

True to his name, my boy is king: he sits astride his mount and lumbers off into the forest. For an hour or more, he's an elephant-boy aboard his beast. These ancient, noble creatures do their work, pulling up trees, transporting logs. Stephen takes a final slide down the trunk of his new-found four-footed friend before she rejoins her family, plunging into the mud for a well-earned bath.

We have a couple of weeks exploring Bangkok before a trip up North, far away from the smog. There's another week to come, beside the sea, swimming, riding in glass-bottomed boats to gaze at the magical world of coral and waving sea-fronds, the warm rocks and glamorously-clad fish that light up the water landscape beneath us. Everywhere we go there's colour, strident and unashamed: colour like I've never seen in my wildest dreams. We feast on the juice of fresh oranges and coconuts; exotic fruits fill our bellies and our eyes.

Time's up soon enough – sooner than we'd like, but there are two sisters waiting back at home. Like angels peeping through the cracks of our rotting mansion, some friendly neighbours have shown up from nowhere and taken these children in as guests. So we're laden with the gifts of paradise as we head off to the airport and the long ride home. It feels as though we've been gone a year or more but it's not cold – just greyish and rather damp – and we're not complaining; we've had the holiday of a lifetime.

South gives way to North, though, and East returns to West. I'm beginning to miss those bright hues already, and we're not even back at the farm. Those colours – how do I say it? – they set your soul alight. Maybe the floaty-people at the Old Manor know something that I've not discovered yet. There has been something deep in this Eastern experience, a glimpse of a life whose inner tapestry makes sense. We shall not forget the richness and the warmth; we'll hold it in our hearts.

But we're turning the corner now, into the drive, and I feel a sinking in my gut. It's the hobgoblins again. I feel them lurking in the stables, in the walls, in my cells. They know we're home and they're not joking any more.

"Breathe deep, you guys," they say. "Drink in those rays of

light and nourishment; ingest them all you can. Feel the warmth and store it up. You ain't seen nothin' yet."

7

Spring 1992

Somehow or other, we've survived another year – the whole of it. But I'm maybe just a little more than half-awake these days. I'm looking for something. It would be an exaggeration to say that I'm searching for God.

A wizard would be more the thing: someone with a handy wand; someone who will take me by the hand and say, "Congratulations, kid – you've done great. And hey, I've got a travelling balloon; it's full of hot air. I'm headed your way; wanna lift? Climb in; bring the kids along. You'll be home in no time."

So I wouldn't say I'm encountering God, exactly, a year on from our respite in the Far East with all its temples, though I'm in the village church right now, it's true. That's where you'll find me most mornings these days – except you won't, probably, because I'm tucked away beneath the altar.

I don't *want* you to find me. I used to like people, back in those blissful days when I had home and warmth and friends. Not now; not any more. Anger and resentment and helplessness are shrinking my mind, closing the doors of my heart as they shut down my cells, squeezing out love and empathy – for all except my precious kids.

I wait until the last of the faithful have departed from morning service before I creep up the church path and push open the heavy door. Then I head straight for my hot spot. I'm sitting cross-legged in a space just large enough to hold me, sheltered from any other prayerful seekers by the thickly embroidered altar-cloth that reaches right down to the floor. It's a perfect child's hideout.

I don't know a lot about prayer. Sunday Mass was mandatory, of course, when I was young, a grim enough affair. I'd tug at my mother's skirt as often as I dared and ask, "How much longer?

When can we go home?"

Ah, home – the eternal question. Maybe the search has been on for longer than I thought.

"Not long now," my mother would whisper back.

I loved the incense, I will say that. I still do. And sometimes, depending on the season or the agenda of the organist aloft, I loved the music.

As for prayer, though, I didn't get it. Apologies for unworthiness and innate wickedness seemed to form a large ingredient, though it was never clear what I'd done wrong. Regular visits to a little dark box would rubber stamp these words of contrition: apparently the man in the dark, the other side of that metal grid, would wipe your slate so you came out squeaky clean. If you couldn't come up with a plausible list of offences it was easy enough: the prayer book had a handy page-full of possible sins.

Keep it simple, though; stay with the ones you know – the ones about late arrivals or stolen jam. The more exotic ones, those abstract phrases you found at the back of the prayer book to ring the changes and relieve the boredom, could land you in very tricky conversations, way above your head. They went something like this:

"Bless me Father, for I have sinned."

"Yes, my child?"

"Um, I pinched my brother (*he was being horrible to me, he deserved it*). I ate two chocolates when we were allowed just one. I had impure thoughts."

Deathly silence.

"Oh, my child…"

What have I said?

"Impure thoughts?" repeats the priest in alarm. "Tell me, my child. What thoughts were these?"

I'm sorry I haven't a clue. Now I feel *properly* guilty, because I've told a fib. I thought that the 'impure thoughts' one was a novelty less repetitive than the stolen sweets and acts of simple disobedience that I'd repeated by rote on previous visits: those were tedious and not even true, a mere fiction cooked up to satisfy my mother and the priest. I had to find some sins from somewhere and now my strategy is blowing up in my face. What are impure thoughts, anyway? The priest seems mightily interested in them.

He talks on, asking me questions. I'm digging myself into a deeper and deeper hole. There's nowhere to go. I'm chicken; I turn tail, push the door and run back to my mother's skirts.

It's called Confession, this charade – and in truth it was not I who picked out 'impure thoughts', it was my friend Noelle, growing up in the depths of rural France: I've borrowed her story for the comic value that my confessional visits sadly lacked. I used the list, though, over and over, and emerged time and again with the guilt of my elusive sins branded firmly on my heart. And just as firmly branded was my intention to steer clear of those dark boxes the minute my legs grew long enough.

They were long ago, these scenes; they're ghosts of memories, nothing more. So what am I doing here, squatting beneath the altar, chatting away to a God I either hate or don't believe in – or both? Only time will tell, because right here, right now, as I squat in the village church, some kind of prayer is just what I need. Not through anyone else, mind you; I'm not looking for intercession. God forbid that the Vicar ever find me here in my hideout, or the woman shuffling around on quiet feet as she refreshes the vases of flowers mere inches from my back, separated from me only by the comforting thickness of the hanging fabric. I'm not keen to be labelled as the village idiot, whatever the state of my mind.

Rather than the casual opinion of the villagers, though, it's people-avoidance that is highest on my agenda right now.

As I withdraw from the world, despair oozes through my veins like silt. But I'm sure she's a kindly woman, this flower person just behind me, and I don't want to give her the fright of her life any more than I wish to be discovered in my den. I wait with bated breath, willing her to go away.

My hot spot, for some reason or other, feels like a special place: maybe it's my childhood conditioning, telling me that proper prayers happen in church. Or maybe it's something else... I know nothing of the history of this small church: for all I'm aware, it may have been wrenched from the hands of Rome centuries ago, in a violent move by those early protesters as humankind pushed out and away from the tentacles of control that had spread through the Middle Ages, and towards the realization of its Self. I've no idea what scenes of conflict and strife these walls may have witnessed in their time, but I sense an energy of something that really isn't fear.

I may be searching for a wizard, but in a little while, further down the line, I shall begin to find that God slips through the spaces.

Above me is a smallish window; the light streams in through its stained and decorated panes. Many people have returned again and again to the quiet peacefulness contained within these stone walls. Like me, perhaps they've asked for something, begged for their heart's desire:

"Please God, take away my pain – or his, or hers."

"Ask," I hear, like a faint echo from the deep past, "and it shall be given unto you. Knock, and the door shall be opened."

Those words have logged themselves somewhere in my heart. All right, dear Mother, maybe that early listening to the Gospels, enforced on mornings when I feigned stomach aches or fever, has left just a little legacy after all.

I can't pretend I believe the words but I'm sitting here all the same; and every day I come back and repeat my own prayer, my cry: "Please, God, help us. Please help us all."

It's a primitive prayer, mine, but maybe it's a beginning. We're wired up to wish for pleasure and to avoid the suffering of pain, so perhaps it's a good starting point, this urgent cry from an ego that's lost, bewildered and confused. If prayer is talking to God, then even if this is a prayer from my child-self – that part of me that feels helpless and abandoned – right here, right now, in my hidey-hole under the ancient altar built of solid stone, something feels a fraction gentler, a shade safer.

Just for the moment, I almost believe that God or the Universe is benevolent and kind. I'm feeling that this mighty force is listening – he, she or it.

The child-self is good at talking, of course; it's not so good at listening. That is the stuff of meditation and in order to pay such attention to God – like truly listening to anyone – I shall need to be still. But I don't know anything about that; I am nowhere *near* to being still, not yet.

So that will have to come later. But just for the moment, dear God – if ever, whoever, wherever you may be – please hear my prayer.

It's an impossible request, this prayer of mine; it's ludicrous, and I've already lost my faith in most of what surrounds me. But I still believe in miracles.

8

Journeys into prayer

There's plenty for this battered ego of mine to pray about. Because the year that has passed by the time I've made it to my church Wendy-house has hardly been a comfortable one. I'll spare you the details; I will only say that from the depths of my brain-fog I really don't have the faintest idea of how or why we ended up in this outrageous place, our special-edition Siberia.

It's turned out that the fields my Outward Bounder dreamed of for so many years have served simply for insulation. These eighteen acres have stood between him and the nearest person, but what do you do with all that land once you've got it? He has racked his brains and come up with the only answer he can find: let them out to a local farmer.

Be careful what you wish for, you might get it. That's how the phrase goes, and the evidence of its truth is hitting us daily now, right in the face. Take care, the phrase means; stay alert, be awake; be mindful of the way you think and speak. We are co-creators all; our thoughts and words boomerang back to us as the reality of our lives: bang, bang, bang.

He's Mount Etna on legs, Mr Paratrooper, always ready to erupt. And we're scared.

The horses have gone. We can't afford to feed ourselves, let alone the beasts of the field. I've made seven more visits down south to oust the squatters, the old home degenerating further with every fresh attack. The notices declaring that this highly desirable residence is *For Sale* have come and gone so many times the local neighbourhood know the place is jinxed: not a single buyer has walked through the door in months.

And my daughter, my first-born, my beloved angel, is three-quarters of the way to a full breakdown. I've tried three different schools for her, each one more devastating than the last. It's not the schools, of course; no single school is more fatally flawed than another.

She's an organism that's been torn from its natural habitat and thrown on to stony ground. Her digestive canal is a fast-running river, a torrent that gives her no rest. She's done the brave face – full-on, and on – until it has finally crumpled in hopelessness. Depression envelops her like a shroud and she can scarcely make it down the stairs. Dispossessed and traumatized, she's now become the dumping ground for her father's rage.

But if I'm Dorothy, she is the Cowardly Lion: right now, she doesn't believe she can do it, any of it; but I know that she can do it and more.

Given a leg up, a gentle push forward, she has the courage to do life with abundant grace and power. She needs a miracle and she's worth it. So something must be done and I know what it is. She had a school in Oxford, she was deeply happy there: a fee-paying establishment, beyond our means even back then. But even then, also, it was the place that kept her safe and I know she must return. We have to find that Wizard.

If her attendance at the old school was an over-pricey solution in the past, this new plan is fully mad. It's obvious to a simpleton that there's no way of returning to live in our old home town; the house there is about to be repossessed and we haven't two farthings left to rub between us. Conjuring up every next meal is an act of faith.

I have written to the headmistress, though, requesting a place for Nicola for the coming September. And now it's May; I have a few months to dream up my action plan. That's why I'm sitting in my hot spot. It's why I'm talking to God. A month or two back, I had no response to the scene more useful than tears. Some generous relatives had taken pity on us, thank Heaven and them, and gifted us with a connection to the mains. Water, wonderful water, now came gushing from our taps. But I could still compete with them and win. I could cry for England.

Not now, though: the tears are spent. I'm silent on my stone seat on the floor, I'm begging for divine intervention. I may be dried-up, bewildered, shrivelled, contracted and full of rage, but I'm not dead yet.

I'm seeing this precious child safely re-established and surrounded by those girls back there who love her: they're still writing to her every other week. Already, perhaps, I'm learning the essence of something closer to real prayer than I've known in the past. I'm not expecting God to do this mighty task, to engage the forces of the Universe in an act that looks impossible, all on his own. I'll help, I promise.

Somehow, through a force of instinct that comes from an ancient place inside my heart and soul, I know that the only way I can help is to hold the vision. I have to do it, so I'll be a good shepherd to my thoughts and words: I'll cherish the good ones, heal the others. And I *will* hold the vision. I'll hold it with every imaginative act I can muster.

But I'm living on Planet Earth and it's a place where we must vote with our hands and our feet. "OK God, you do your part, I'll do mine."

So it's action time. Step one: I write to Michael Jackson, Nicola's great comforter and hero. I assure him that if only he will come to our aid and rescue my child she will be worth it, she really will: she too will *heal the world*, for all she's worth. Step two: I gather up the trinkets I've been given by kindly ancestors, small pieces of silver and gold. I take Magdalen, the little one, with me – she's five now – and we set off for London's jewel markets, stopping off in Wembley on the way. Jackson's concert is in a day or two and "yes," the scaffold man assures me, "he will get my letter delivered to the right place." I could hug him.

So how much are my jewels worth? A few hundred pounds. And the school fees? Ten thousand a year, give or take a pound or two.

I go through the same charade with my antique furniture: a glass bookcase, a Georgian paper-knife, a chest of drawers. And then I step up my efforts. I've got it – the football pools! Twice every week. That'll do it, that's the answer – if there's a merciful God out there. *Please!!*

Mr Paratrooper has learned my plot, and sneers in disgust and disbelief. "You've no sense of responsibility," he says. "Write to the school and own up. The whole hare-brained scheme is nothing but a lie."

But I don't believe him. And there's something else: I've been spending time with the floaty people at the Old Manor. And it's not just the central heating that's drawn me into its wacky warmth: I've been making friends. I find I want to brush my lips and cheeks with hints of pink and even whisk some shape into my hair. This is not doing the marriage any good, but with each passing week I care a little less. Besides, I've met someone there who does that now-interesting weird stuff; he makes birth charts for you, based on configurations of the stars, and he tells you wonderful things. He's called William.

"Will Nicola return to her safe haven?"

I've asked my new friend William this question several weeks ago, long before the latest eruption from Etna.

"Oh yes, she very likely will," he has replied.

"So I'm not mad?"

"You're not. She needs it, she deserves it; it seems she's going to get it. It looks like something is going to happen at the end of July. We're often not given the means, the mechanism. But don't cancel that place you've reserved – she'll be needing it."

I may not know it yet but the angels are lining up. They're watching and hovering, and they're about to land.

9

On magic and miracles

Before the angels have a place to land, though, I have work to do: I have to clear a space in my mind, my psyche, my heart. Perhaps I have to clear a space in my life.

There was an epiphany the other night – long overdue – when I woke at that starry-lucid time of three o'clock, and found myself lying beside the man I had once decided to marry. With stark clarity, I knew I could not spend another moment with him in the same room. This was the brutal, inescapable truth: denial was no longer an option.

"I'm sorry, Mr Outward Bound, I really am."

I'm speaking silently into the pitch dark, inching my way out of the bed, quietly lifting the covers.

"I can't live with you," I continue, "not for thirty seconds more. A few years from now I shall be doing quite an arctic hike in learning to live with my *self*, but I don't know that yet. There's a pain inside me that's just a bit bigger than I am and I can't hack it any more; I can't hack being in the same place that you are, or even within a mile of it. I'm sorry that I feel this hostility and disgust and all this dark satanic rage, because even now I'm feeling compassion and sadness too.

"Please don't take it personally. I mean it's personal, of course; it's about a marriage after all. I mean I know I can't stand you and everything but you know really I'm quite fond of you and I'd love you to have a nice life. I know you're a walking disaster but you're talented and very clever."

Oh dear this is coming out all wrong. The man's fast asleep and even now I'm just a few yards down this road called communication practice and I've hit spaghetti junction *already*. My tongue's all twisted and my brain is a fog. It's almost as scary as talking to my father.

Ah, that would be it then. But I'm feeling stronger now, clearer, as I edge away from the bed and the space around me grows.

"It's what happens in a marriage," my silent monologue continues, "when you suppress your truth; and it happens in life too. In a marriage, it's comparatively simple. The pressure builds inside until the lid flips right into the ocean; you get a tsunami, a tidal wave. It sweeps away everything in its path. In life, it's not always so obvious. It turns into heart disease, cancer, terminal despair."

And now I'm speaking to someone else: God, perhaps.

"Please make him telepathic. Please make him understand. It's not only me that I'm setting free, or his precious children. It's him, too."

I'm out of the bedroom; I've crept away into the silence of the night. Um, where do I go now? This house keeps up its arrangement with the ice-fairies all year round. Bobble hats, gloves and several layers of sweaters: these are our regular nightwear but I've also crawled out from beneath five layers of bedcovers and I'm shivering already.

So what shall I do next, in this place with its crumbling walls and its rough wooden-or-concrete floors? Ah! - it's not only water that we have these days; there's an ancient Aga stove in the kitchen. As long as you keep it well topped up with logs and coal, it will deposit a film of fine black dust over everything in the house and it will also – God bless its roaring belly – provide lashings of hot water, day and night. It's my new best friend.

I pad silently down the stairs and run a deep, deep ocean of water into the Stone-Age tub. There are four hours before the alarm clocks will tell us it's time to tackle another day. That gives me plenty of thinking time. I'm finding that my church hideout is not the only spot where I can pursue my chats with the Team Upstairs. This Prayer thing is becoming something of a habit.

I've not had an answer yet to the Nicola conundrum, but I'm deeply, steadily optimistic. I've never been more certain in my life.

Nor have I ever been so sure of the action I must take that's just as close to home as this – or moving just as far away from it. I must leave, I must go away, I must quit. I don't know when I'll do it; I certainly don't know how. I haven't a bean left in all the world and no clear means to find one. I've never had less security in my life. But I will do it. And it will be soon.

It's a proper baptism, this bath. It's washing away the sins of the fathers and mothers, their sons and daughters all. The fear, the remnants of indecision, the unbelief – I'm watching as it sloshes down towards the great gully beneath. I'll rescue these children of mine, if it's the last thing I do. I'll rescue them from the sins of *their* fathers and *their* mothers, those sins that are spiralling out and down to earth, right through the drain. What's a sin anyway? Oh yes, that's right – it's when we miss the mark. Have to keep practising, try again: I'll do better in future, I promise.

And fear, what's that? Well, just look at the acronym: Forgetting Everything's **A**ll **R**ight. So how about you just don't forget any more? OK, then, it's all fine, just fine. I'm ready for anything; I'll do whatever it takes. Kids, we're invincible: let's start over.

Comment

Marriage and the Ego

Retrospective lenses can give us the super-clear sight that we rarely have at the moment that we're living some part of our life journey – particularly a tricky one. Later, when we look over our shoulder to the past, in one sense we see it for the first time. We've stepped off the stage; we've gained a little distance.

Here I was, in the process of saying goodbye to Mr Outward Bound, and at the time I had no idea why we'd spent sixteen years under the same roof, while there still was one. I didn't even *want* to think too much when I was still on the farm, with animals to feed and stables to muck out. That was surely no time for contemplation.

Or was it? Maybe this is the whole point: maybe we'd grow a whole lot faster if we paid attention in the instant when our lives are happening most intensively all around us. "Before enlightenment, push wheelbarrow move manure. After enlightenment, etc." Maybe the key that unlocks the door to enlightenment has less to do with what we do and more to do with how we do it.

If I'd been ready to listen to divine guidance, or the still small voice of the inner self, or any voice at all that was not drowned by the cacophony inside my head, in those last months on the farm before the horses left, before *we* left; as I heaved manure and dug the soil, planting shrubs which never stood a chance against the force of those everlasting winds; if I'd opened my ears to the messages that the Universe works to post through the resistant walls of our psyche, they might have gone something like this:

"You're standing there in deep shit – it's heavy work; a good time for reflection. How about thanking the horse for pushing you to move some heavy karmic loads? D'you think you might be purifying your ego, reducing its gravitational force as you dust it off and lighten it up?

"You're fertilizing the arid earth of this place, the horses and you; you're nourishing the daffodils and apple trees. Perhaps you're nourishing something way beyond all this; perhaps your energy-field will soak up the fertilizer; maybe it will grow and glow."

No, my ears and eyes were a long way from any such imagery or abstract thought. Nor did I want to think about the marriage I was working so hard to leave behind. I just wanted out, with the minimum of wounds and hard feelings. Sixteen years... But now, with the support of hindsight, I know that nothing is ever wasted.

Two people don't set out to hurt each other; I guess that's fairly obvious. And of course, there are two people in every partnership: that's obvious too. So I'm most certainly not all good – self-evident enough – and Mr Paratrooper is not all bad: a little less self-evident at the time, at least to me.

We started out, years back along the road, though, with great hopes and intentions. We were kids, of course, and no-one was there to stop us.

Ah, but there shouldn't be anyone there to stop us: this is the first thing that hindsight makes perfectly clear.

Our life path is a set-up, a journey that's largely pre-planned, and we're the ones who wrote the script and drew the map. The path is a road drawn through the ongoing scenery of our lives, or the stage props that are set up by our souls. It winds and twists and doubles back on itself and it leads us to the very heart of ourselves.

We don't walk this road alone, though: we hook up with fellow travellers along the way; we form connections, we forge relation-ships.

Moreover, those relationships are the perfect – perhaps the only – place through which we human people come to find the selves that we're seeking. We see those selves, or parts of them, reflected in the mirrors around us: mirrors which consist of each other, on the one hand, and on the other hand the conditions we create through the interactions that we have with one another. As often as not, when we catch sight of those mirrors, we don't like what we see. But then I hate to say it: that's how we get to grow up.

Mr Outward Bound and I knew none of that in our twenties, of course. Press the fast-forward button, move a few decades on, to somewhere in our forties, perhaps, for even a beginning of this understanding, because the teens and twenties are the time when ego's in charge, a tricky, subtle thing if ever there was one. The ego comes from the mind; it's the wily little part of us that thinks we're separate.

Don't get me wrong: the ego is vital and one of the first mistakes we make as we become alerted to its presence is to judge it and then to attempt to get rid of it. No, it's the vehicle that gets us out there, into the world; it's a crucial part of the set-up.

We have to find a sense of ourselves as individual beings or we would never get anything done. Without a sense of our physical boundaries we'd be in danger of our lives; without emotional boundaries our relationships would be in permanent meltdown. There has to be a who-I-am before we can put our contribution into the what-we-are, and the only route to authentic, soul-based power is through the development of our individual, ego-based power.

The author and teacher Ram Dass expresses it in language that's simple and strong: "We must first be a somebody, before we are ready to be a nobody."

The fact, despite all of this, is that it's a tightrope the ego has to walk. It is a job for it to find balance and stay there because while we're in it, in this journey of apparent separation through the experience of a body and a mind, that sense of separation or isolation feels completely real, so, like any energy body, this little entity is terrified of extinction: if it doesn't puff itself up, it thinks it's in danger of starvation. So it tells us, "You're on your own, mate, but don't you worry. I'll look after you. Trust me."

The ego may tell us we're great: cleverer than one person, kinder than another; richer than him, prettier than her; the coolest kid on the block. It might tell us we're witty and generous and thoroughly to be admired.

If it does, it's because it doesn't believe a word of it, or because – even if any of this looks true on the surface – none of it makes us feel safe on the inside. Really, the ego feels very small, which is hardly surprising. It is.

So the other way the ego works is to tell us this directly: "You're not too bright, are you? Not very resourceful; under-qualified; slow to learn. Pity you didn't get yourself a decent job and a higher salary, but then you don't deserve a life as good as the beautiful people over there. And you'll never get that anyway, of course – it's not in your genes, your stars. Poor you, you've suffered so much, but never mind: that's what makes you special."

And on, and on, swinging one way, swinging another, never coming very near the centre; that's too close to the heart. It's the danger zone, the heart; the place that invites us to expand and connect.

It reminds us of what we have forgotten: that we're all equal; we're all the same stuff. The heart warms up our lives and guides us to our souls. This is not what the ego wants at all: it will positively dissolve in all that warmth, get lost in all that space.

"No-one will notice me; no-one will feed me!" the ego screams. "How will I survive?"

So the ego stays contracted, where it feels safe. In its doomed efforts to grow, let alone make it through the day, it gorges on fear, the only food it knows, and it grabs hold of us by the hand.

"Let's hang out," it says, "or hang in. You stay right here with me."

That's pretty much where most of us are, as we approach our so-called adult lives. We have our legacies, our baggage, a cartload of anxiety and trepidation and stress, deeply hidden and filtering our true perception.

It's been handed down from the last lot of adults, who got it from the lot before that, who got it from the lot before that: the generations of parents and teachers groping their way through their own confusion as they navigate life on planet earth. And because the baggage is deeply hidden, we have no idea that this is what is going on. We're under 30, under 40, vital force is high. *We* are high, perhaps: we've found our prince, our hunk, our goddess; they gave us the job, we got the house, the car, the toys.

So, somehow or other, through a process that went something like the one I've just described, I found myself long ago with Mr Outward Bound and he – poor fellow – found himself with me. He should have married a paratrooper and I should have married a – what? Perhaps I'll discover that later. More than this: he should have *been* a paratrooper, for real, for good, and I should have *been* a – what? Perhaps I'll discover that later as well.

For the moment, I did what my parents expected; I embraced the only profession that would get their stamp of approval in a dozen lifetimes: it was called marriage. Mr Outward Bound fell in love, in need, in something anyway; and so, after a fashion, did I. Just for the time being, we both believed we'd found someone who got us: we were both trying to do life in the only way that appeared to present itself in the light of the filters bestowed on our perception by the respective packages we carried. What's more, we were scared of doing it on our own.

"You just stay in here with me," our egos said to one another. "We'll make out together. It'll be safer that way."

So – like egos right across the planet – ours bonded together, and built their structure; they made their homes. How could they know their constitution was so fragile; are we even meant to know that our houses are made of cards and built on sand? Better, perhaps, that we learn this slowly, one little piece at a time.

A moment or two later, then, or so it seemed, Mr Outward Bound and I had underpinned our frail structure with a mortgage. And then we were filling it with - one, two, three – children, and he was stuck in a job he loathed.

It was not long before those egos of ours stopped feeding one another with fast food, or any food at all. They were corroding one another instead; they were scratching away at each other in their effort to survive. That is what egos do: stranded in their illusion of separateness, they don't know any other way.

The scratching doesn't necessarily look like scratching, of course: maybe it looks like asking one another for more than the other can provide; maybe it's projecting one's despondency on to another. It may take the form of subtle put-downs, manipulation or control. However it happens, the upshot is much the same: confidence, self-belief, faith, optimism, hope: they all evaporate, slowly, quietly. We hardly even notice where they went.

But let's not be too hasty; let's not make the ego bad and wrong. Because all of that process of dissolution has to be a good thing, in the end.

One way or another, our egos in their primitive state must be dismantled, in order that they can evolve and transform into their greater, truer essence.

When Socrates said that the unexamined life is not worth living, he was right. He might have added that the unexamined life is dangerous: the unexamined ego is the stuff of war. That's why the journey to the heart isn't an optional extra: it's what we have to embark on if we intend to survive.

In order to get there, to find that heart place, most often through the relationships we find ourselves embarked on, there's another little thing in the mix: it's called karma. There's something in our relationships – often in the most challenging ones – that we have contracted to work out; to clear out and understand. This is something, perhaps, from our childhoods, our family legacies, our gene pools even; something from the deep, forgotten past.

I know little of this yet, as I sweep up the remains of sixteen years' existence and prepare to walk off into the unknown. I scarcely know I have an ego, or rather that it has me. If you ask me even what the ego *is*, I'll be lost for a convincing reply.

I'm not ready for too much introspection, but I'm no longer, perhaps, completely asleep.

There's work to be done: it's time to move out of the passenger seat, away from that long-familiar default setting of the life I've allowed, and take out the map, the keyboard, the steering wheel – any of those tools we find hidden away inside when we're ready to look – and claim them for myself.

Two

Miracle: an extraordinary and welcome event
believed to be the work of God or a saint

10

Summer 1992

The long break has just begun and the two older children are invited to France, rescued by two young friends in an old umbrella car. The four of them have set off, luggage bandaged to the roof and reaching for the sky, to spend the next six weeks in the Mediterranean sun.

Magdalen is still young; she will stay home and we'll make out together. We shall spend a quiet summer getting ready for the changes ahead.

Nicola rings me every third day or so, asking what I've heard from Michael Jackson and my other friends. "Hang in there," I tell her.

The postman delivers a card through the door. The message is simple buy mysterious: a one-liner. "Don't worry," it reads. "Help is in sight!"

It's come from a distant cousin; I scarcely know her. We have met once or twice before, in the dim past, that other lifetime when our existence was dull and wonderfully safe.

She was fond of my parents and would visit every seven years on sabbatical leave from her teaching post in a North American university. With my parents now long-deceased, she's not in touch with anyone who knows me. I wonder vaguely how she even has my address. Maybe I've been a little more thorough with the Christmas cards than I remembered. Anyhow, here's the note and she's inviting herself to stay, please, almost at once. Will I fetch her from the station?

I do so, of course. It's a twenty-mile drive from the farm. She doesn't hang about, this woman. She's here with her bombshell and she drops it the moment we're in the car and headed back for Wuthering Heights.

"You remember that opal bracelet?" she asks.

I don't. She reminds me that she showed it to me seven years ago and tells me that it's been held since then by a jeweller in London. "I asked him to sell it the other day," she goes on, "just before I left. And to send the cash to you. It should fetch quite a bit."

"*What?*"

I'm dumbfounded, stunned – and even more so as my brain cogs kick into action, because today is the second day of August and William the Astrologer has said that something will happen at the end of July. Just four or five days ago, my cousin issued her instructions to sell. The simple calculation flashes through my brain: four or five days ago was the 28th or 29th of July.

I'm driving: hold it steady, girl. I tell Patricia a chapter or two of our recent story. Above all, I tell her of Nicola's trials and our mad, sure, crazy, certain hope against hope.

"Ah," she says. "You mustn't sell that bracelet in a hurry. If our man finds the right buyer, it will pay the first year's fees and maybe more."

We're back in the kitchen now, with its derelict walls and broken doors. But for once, the sun has popped out from behind its usual veil of clouds and the winds have taken an hour or two's break. I'm making tea and carrying it into the garden – well, the field. Patricia has pulled out her cheque book and written a cheque, direct to the school, covering the first term's fees.

What can I give her? What can you possibly give to the person who saves the life of your child? Nothing, of course, save gratitude and a little companionship: a guided tour of the local scenery, really quite picturesque in full summer. A close-up of the cathedral and its cobbled streets; a comprehensive sweeping of every shop and den that offers antiquities for sale.

And now it's evening and the phone is ringing. It's Nicola, again. "Any news from Michael Jackson?"

"Oh, there's something way better than that. An angel just

arrived and she's standing right here in the kitchen. She's paid your school fees for September. It's done, you're going back home – so relax now and enjoy the lake." The screams of joy and relief race down the line and reverberate around us. For once, even the sad walls of this place have altered their mood.

As things turn out, Patricia is right about her priceless jewel. A few months later, as Nicola is settling back into her old haven of safety and peace, the man from London gets in touch. The bracelet has been sold for eleven thousand pounds. Nor will this be the end of it, because a few months later we hear again from this unexpected person. She's taken a decision, she says: she'll see Nicola through the next five years, until the end of school.

Just for the moment, then, against odds so impossible they boggle your mind, this child is home and dry. And years later, I will tell this extraordinary story to one of my cousin's closest friends, an academic like herself.

"What prompted you to come so spectacularly to their aid?" he will ask her.

"Oh," she will say quietly. "Just some kind of instinct."

She's a Professor, this woman, deeply rooted in the world of logic and pure reason. Those people do empiricism and facts, not the world of messages floating out from the ethers, that nebulous ocean of whispers so subtle they pass us by, unheard. That's what I've always understood, but things are rarely what they seem. The world is full of mystery and magic and more often than not, the answer to prayer comes from the last place we expect. Thank you, Pat.

11

September 1992

Goodbye, Wuthering Heights. I have left and I shall not miss you. Our first stop is a borrowed caravan; but that's while it's still summer, thank heaven. For the next stop, as term starts again, the three of us lodge in the spare bedroom of a long-suffering friend, long weeks on end. Nicola has already left; she's settling back into the life the rest of us are still waiting for.

Now a few months later, as the last leaves are falling, we have a place to rent. There's not a cent left to our name but mercifully this country has a political system founded partly on a central tenet that's handy for us: the poor shall not starve – not quite. I don't have a bank account and I certainly don't have a credit card, but I have a new kind of structural safety net, a simple routine that's reassuring in its novel economy: every Monday morning the woman behind the post office counter will hand me eight notes, each worth ten pounds. That makes £4,160 p.a. to share between the four of us.

Thank you, Universe: this is *way* better than starvation. It's way better than the deep freeze, come to that, because guess what – this place has central heating. I will use my ten-pound notes to feed and clothe us, to cover the cost of travel, phone, heating. When I calculate that the meal we just ate cost nine pence a portion, the children raise their hands and cheer. It's easy: lentils, cabbage and rice.

It's a funny thing, money. Before we arrived in this new and unfamiliar state, I've always thought of it as a finite substance. I've believed it to be a solid kind of a thing with no flexibility at all. You have it or you don't; you are born into a family that's rich, poor or somewhere in the middle. Some people may get a lucky break but the chances are that most of us will just muddle along.

In my case, of course, I'm wrong; muddling along hasn't turned out to be the deal after all – far from it. We're cleaned right out and starting over.

Here we are then, but we're managing just about on our 80 pounds a week income, while Mr Paratrooper staggers by on 42,000 a year, fuming.

We're shell-shocked, it's true, but we're generally rather happier than we've been for some time. And we are discovering something we never knew before: there is nothing firm or fixed about money. Somehow or other, with a fraction of the funds that have been available in the past, we're having more fun than we used to. There's an Indian food house in the local cathedral town: we fill ourselves on curry and still pocket the change from one of our precious ten-pound notes. There's a great treat for an occasional Saturday, and we shall soon find all kinds of others.

Perhaps money is as fluid and intangible as the rest of this strange new world that seems to be replacing my old certainties. Perhaps – like everything else I've been learning about, money is really nothing but energy either, picking up our thoughts and throwing them back at us as something more tangible, like a swelling bank account if we're happy or a notice to quit if we're stressed out.

Well, it's an interesting idea; it provokes me to question and thought, and it will pose ongoing challenges and tests in the years ahead. Our heads can often grasp a concept swiftly and easily; our bodies, on the other hand, remember the traumas and the shocks.

"Just think it see it," you tell them, with your new-found evangelism.

"Yeah right," they reply, shaking their cells in mild ridicule.

It's Friday, three weeks on, time to collect Nicola from Oxford and spend a weekend at home. It's a three to four-hour drive. She's asking about Wispa, her precious dog. We had to leave her at the farm because there's no room in the cottage to swing a cat, let alone a bouncing Collie who likes to run twenty miles a day.

Besides, the road outside is far too dangerous. But the two of them belong to each other; they're deeply bonded.

"She's OK," I'm telling Nicki. "I walk her every day. I make sure it's well over in the opposite direction to the new place – they're about a mile apart. We must make sure she doesn't see where we're living, it would be too cruel."

We roll up to the front door at last, and it's dark; it must be gone ten o'clock. We reach the front doorstep, and who is sitting there? You've probably guessed it: "OK Wispa," I say, "you win. You'll obviously have to come and stay."

How did she know where we live? And how did she know Nicola was coming home that day? Research into the psychic powers of animals is only in its early stages; we know very little as yet. (If you're interested, read Rupert Sheldrake's *Dogs that Know When their Owners are Coming Home*, Three Rivers Press 2000, and The Language of *Miracles* by Amelia Kinkade, New World Library.) It's certainly more than probable that animals, like children, carry less baggage than we do; they have less mind-stuff cluttering up their perception. So in a way they are more alert, more sensitive than we are; they're far more finely tuned. They are more immediately responsive to the way that energy travels in an invisible world that is very much more dynamic than we've guessed.

As these adventures of my own small tribe unfold, the force of energy is what we shall be calling on more than once or twice in order to save our very skins, but in fact, all of humankind draws on this force every moment of every day – not just in moments of crisis or pain, not just when we're working to create some kind of conscious change, but in the simplest things: our breathing, our thinking, our feeding; and in every interaction with one another that we ever make.

Right now, though, as I'm arranging our few possessions in the new cottage, I'm grateful for energy in a simpler and more familiar form. The cottage may be small but it's comfortable, and that holy grail of all treasures, the central heating, is a relief way beyond imagination. There are carpets too – and walls with plaster and paint. Taps that work; built-in cupboards; there's even a dishwasher.

Winter is around the corner again, but we can face it with a smile. Life is beginning to feel almost peaceful: even my youngest child is settling into her primary-school class just around the corner.

School in the morning, then, and a few spare hours available for study. I can glimpse a time, not so far off now, when I shall start putting some healing skills to practise. I studied homoeopathic medicine, after all, back in Oxford.

I spent years doing massage and a kind of spiritual healing, doing what came naturally to my hands: it's the work I like to do. I'm well up for swelling the cash flow, too; ready to spruce up our diet of lentils and rice.

It's hot chocolate all round, then and a good night's sleep.

12

A few days later

John Lennon was right – Life is without a doubt the thing that happens when you're busy making other plans.

The peace and quiet lasted three days and then finished with a bang, because I'm in the hospital now, walking along beside my bed-ridden son. He's just been wheeled out of the operating theatre. Very sudden; very scary.

He arrived in my bed in the early hours, the third night in our little haven of warmth and peace.

"I can't hack this pain," he said. Stephen's the one who never complains about physical pain: he'd have to be dying before he'd let you know about it. So I should have known, I should have been more alert: the moaning must surely be something like they heard on the battlefields of World War I.

He throws up a few times. I'm reading the situation as best I can. Do I call the doctor or wait till morning? Wait a little longer; I've never been one to bother the physicians in the dead of night. But now, all of a sudden, there's a stream flowing from his backside and it's turned green, oh my God! I should have called the doctor two hours ago. St Michael and all angels – help us, please.

The village doctor arrives at once and promptly calls Emergency. He helps me convert my car to a makeshift ambulance that shoots through twenty miles at breakneck speed to meet the team of medics waiting outside the hospital. Stephen is unconscious: on to a drip and into IT, fast.

"Quick, for heaven's sake, do the operation! Now! What are you waiting for?"

That's me speaking, silent but frantic, chewing my nails and my hair as I look on, helpless. Why are they being so deathly slow? His appendix has burst – the doctor has told me so already. You've got to save his *life. Hurry,* for heaven's sake. The hospital team are not so sure, though: maybe it's the appendix, they say, but it could be kidney failure instead.

"And if it's kidney failure?" I ask, "what then?"

"Oh," says the nurse casually, "he'll have to be on a kidney machine for the rest of his life."

"*What?*"

The minutes pass like weeks as my panic reaches screaming pitch and no-one seems to be doing anything at all. Morning drifts on into afternoon and – still at snail's pace – afternoon turns to evening. But now, at last, they have an answer: yes, it's the appendix. It's exploded like Mount Etna (these sins of the fathers come back to haunt us in the most alarming way). And yes, they will operate at last – at once, in fact. I rush to follow the bed as it's wheeled towards the operating theatre; it's obvious he needs me right beside him to keep him safe. Of course he does, but: "Sorry, no family allowed in theatre."

So off I go in search of a pew in the nearby Cathedral to seek out some of that peace I found in a similar place before; but it's gone five and the place is bolted and barred. It's fish and chips, then, on a bench, as I gaze at the setting sun.

But now I'm back in the hospital as they bring him along the corridor. He's lying there, Egyptian mummy-fashion, with wires hooking various parts of his anatomy to those terrifying hospital machines and a drip. It's been touch and go, they tell me, but he's on his way back to the ward and he's going to be all right.

Thank Heaven and the wonders of medical science. Such lethal poisoning as this is followed by inflammation so severe, though, that morphine must be used to dull the pain: injections into his backside; you can hear the screams right down the corridor.

"Please would you leave off the morphine now?" I beg.

"I'm sorry," says the nurse, "but I'm afraid we can't: it's a decision we have to take. Without it the pain would probably give him a heart attack."

They stop in the end, though, these injections, as the inflammation is gradually becalmed. But so is he: this child is not himself, nowhere near. I'm soon seated beside him and I keep my hands on his belly because I'm hoping to minimize adhesions as well as soothe the pain. He's been my teacher for years, this kid; he's sharp as a razor and he doesn't miss a trick. He's Dorothy's Scarecrow: he sees behind the veil; he spots the solutions; he points the way. I've done energy healing for years, it's instinctive, but he's about to teach me things now that I never knew before.

So when I'm working on him a few days later and some intuition prompts me to move my hands off his skin, a little farther from his body, he speaks. I'm all ears; he's hardly even whispered for days on end.

"Keep your hands like that," he says. "It works better that way. I can feel things moving inside."

I do what I'm told; I keep my hands off his body, eight or ten inches away. So I'm looking at this precious boy and I'm listening for his instructions, clearly given, and I'm thinking that we're pushing out here and maybe getting a little glimpse of new territory. And soon this is confirmed, because it's a few more days on now and the long-suffering medics have tried every trick to revive him: cushions, TV, board games, chicken soup, *ice cream*. And still he falls asleep. He used to do life big-time; not any more.

He's becoming a bit of a legend – and not the good sort. The disconcerted nurses are running out of inspiration as they prop him up once more in a central armchair and yet again he starts to flop. It's time to go at the energy again. They've been teaching me a thing or two, my friends at the Manor. I've shown up for a few visits by now and I've learned the oddest things.

How about this one, for instance? Brace yourself – it's all about the aura and you *can't see it happening*; well, Parvati at the Manor seemed to think she could: "I can see the light behind you," she'd told me, all those months ago. The rest of us – ordinary mortals like me, for instance – have to take it on trust. It's true, as it happens, even truer to say "the light around you;" and just to reassure you, if you're the hard facts type, a high-voltage specialist camera would reveal all. But what is the aura anyway?

It's worth spending a minute or two on this, if you're not already familiar with the concept, since the aura has everything to do with light, and the place that we're heading for – the culmination of the story, if you like – is angelic healing, which also has a great deal to do with light.

So the aura is an extension of yourself, in a manner of speaking. It's your personal energy field, nice and comfortable around you. You'll notice this when someone comes up close, an inch or two from your face: you want to scat.

The ancient schools of acupuncture will explain this to you the other way about – and they've been around for 5,000-odd years so they know a thing or two. They will tell you not so much that the aura sits around you but more that you sit inside *it*; that the aura, in fact, *creates* the you that you know as you: a bright and shiny aura makes a bright and shiny person, health all glowing, but an aura that's congested, dulled or squashed makes for something else.

And all of this is pretty much confirmed by the quantum mechanics; they tell us that the physical world is the end-product of energy. Pure energy comes first, before it condenses down and turns itself into form – trees and flowers and people. To be more specific, the nature of this energy is that it comes from light: this primal substance is the raw material behind pretty much all the life we've ever seen.

If this is the case then we'd do well to give the aura a bit of respect. This nebulous light-field seems to be the light-force, or the life force, which feeds our bodies in all kinds of ways. And light, of course, has a habit of breaking up into all kinds of different colours. So the aura also influences what's happening with our bodies, and tells us a whole lot about what's going on with those bodies (and our minds, come to that, and our spirits, and our hearts).

So right here in the hospital, in this strange situation where I have a post-operative child who is supposed to be getting better after a near-death encounter but is stuck somewhere in limbo-land instead, this is what I do:

I gather up my newly-gleaned knowledge that in near-death or deep shock the human energy field shifts way off balance, that it travels away from its lovely symmetrical arrangement encasing the body and it ends up somewhere out East – or West, depending on which way you're looking at it.

I've learned that it gets stranded there and the shocked and shattered person slumps in a chair or vaguely tries to tackle life something like a chicken without a head, unless and until this bewildered aura is persuaded to come back home.

It may be that there are other ways of coaxing the misplaced energy field back into place, but I've been learning some of the mysterious uses of colour and I have a magic potion in my bag. I spray some into the palms of my hands.

Orange is the thing – it's the most shocking of all the colours and so it understands shock. It's the one that smacks of juicy high-vitality fruits and tropical sunrise but it's also the surrender of autumn leaves or Buddhist monks. I rub it on my hands and get to work.

For the next half hour, if you happen to be wheeling a meal-trolley through this hospital ward or visiting your young friend or relation, you may falter a little, just like those discombobulated farm workers did in the fields back near the farm as they saw the floaty people over the hedge.

This is certainly what the nurses do, as they see me busily waving my hands at thin air (it's not like the church here; there's nowhere to hide), and swishing all that nothingness from the space out West from his ribs, stopping when I get back too near to his pyjamas. Swoosh, swoosh, swoosh, I'm going, for a full half-hour. But then, when Stephen sits up all by himself for the first time in over a week, chatting and laughing for the next eight hours, the trolleys stop dead in their tracks.

You can stop and stare all you like. Stephen is alive and kicking.

13

Bridges of light

I have a new spiritual teacher and he's a proper freak show: rings and necklaces dangling; ear-studs and bracelets, jewels everywhere. He carries tarot cards, rune-stones, crystal-and-feather wands. He sees fairies, goblins, and devas, whatever they may be. And he 'channels' Ascended Masters – ah, them again. Oh yes, and Archangels.

He moves between the worlds and if ever there was evidence that we walk this earth more than once, Mozart and he are it: he's young enough to be my son.

I've just met this young Edwin and he's done a reading for me – a *soul* reading, it's called. He's asked me for the princely sum of five pounds for his services and I've had the spare cash available because I've just set out on the task of supplementing our diet of lentils and cabbage by selling the first volumes from my long-held collection of books. So I'm listening to his tape.

He's talking about light and dark. Wake up, girl, he's saying: there's light out there, all right, the stuff you love to see in all of the people all of the time, but there's darkness too. And yes there's light inside you and around you, the stuff you love to see in all that *you* are all of the time, and there's darkness in there too. Naïve isn't good; it doesn't work in the end.

Wake up and wise up, or the darkness will grab your ankles and pull you into the deep. Face the shadow, the shadows: the ones within your own depths, and those on the outside too. Keep on taking things at face value and you'll fall flat on your face.

"You want dark?" I say. I'm sulking. "I can do dark. I can tell you a thing or two about dark, cold; *all* of it."

"You're a healer," he's telling me, "and you need your box of tools. Embrace them, all of them; and embrace your*self*, all of you.

You can show people the way to their hearts as you discover the path to your own."

I'm hearing the spaces between the lines. No matter what you do, this kid seems to be saying, it's all smoke and mirrors; it's all a reflection of what is happening within.

Reading and studying, that's my thing: the world of books is good and safe. But whether you're reading, studying, travelling, hearing, watching, he seems to suggest, the only thing that matters in the end is that in all our actions and interactions, our journeys and stories, we're learning about ourselves; we're honing our skills for the tasks we've been set. What we see on the outside is merely the dream; a chimera, a reflection of the true reality which is created from the inside.

This is unnervingly similar to some of the things I've been hearing at the Manor. I have a sneaking, rather uncomfortable suspicion that there's something this preposterously young man is pushing me to do: he's telling me to grow up.

"Who am I?" asks the Indian mystic, Ramana Maharshi.

Answer that, the mystic says, and you have the key to the Universe.

And now he's telling me something else, this youngster who's scarcely left his teens. There will be seminars to run, he says, and books to write. As if this weren't absurd enough, he's suggesting there's a new healing system which, at some time in the future, I shall be required to midwife into the world.

It's ridiculous, of course. I'm a lone parent without a bean or a skill that I can put to any serious use in this sparsely-populated county. HM Government pays my rent and there's no passage back from the sticks we live in to the world I knew and loved. My spirit is half-broken at the very least and I have the self-confidence and the manifesting power of a worm. I have little desire to get up in the mornings. If truth be told, I'd much prefer to leave the planet – but it's not an option. I must cherish my kids.

"You're an old soul," he's saying, "in terms of experience. When you come into earth at all, you cram a whole load in all in one go; you do the thing big-time. On the other hand, he adds, you don't come in too often."

"Good decision," I say.

He's talking about Rome. He seems to think I've been there after all.

"I like Rome! – pannaccotta, caffe latte, dolcelatte..."

But the tape is interrupting my stream of thought. Forget the delis, the coffee shops: we're talking a couple of millennia back down the road.

"Ah, but the galleries," I insist. "The paintings; all that lovely stone. And the *clothes.*"

"Sackcloth," the tape replies. "And armour," it adds. "You were a soldier."

"*What?*"

You were a soldier, this young man is saying, but then along came Christ, and his energy seemed more authentic. You started leaving the soldierly escapades behind and your family and friends weren't so chuffed about that – plus they had some hefty weapons.

"Soldierly escapades? That's not me; I'm a peaceful, loving kind of person. Soldierly stuff is Mr Outward Bound's terrain, not mine."

"Oh really?" asks an irritating inner voice.

"Well, yes. It's obvious."

"Then why did you pull confrontation and all the rest of the military stuff into your life? Be a soldier, see a soldier."

The karmic wheel: do something one day and another day you get the credit, or the debit. Do as you would be done by – because you'll get it back anyway, one of these days. This lifetime, next lifetime: don't ask! Don't forget the totality though. Never forget those three young friends of yours – or any others, come to that. You manifested them too.

But there's good news: I'm not alone after all – I've got spirit guides. There's an old man who saved my life when I abandoned the soldierly escapades and followed Christ. He wears sackcloth and he's with me right now, day and night. I look nervously around the room: no faces; no sackcloth, not a breath of wind. There are others too: a native American, a scribe. They'll come and go, apparently, depending on what I'm into, depending what advice I need at the time: they'll take me places, show me things. They're inaudible and invisible, but it seems that this is not a problem. Oh and there's a guardian angel, too, with me for life. The nuns got that bit right, anyway.

Edwin says I'll be needing to meditate. I'm not at all sure about that.

"And I wish you luck and courage," he's finishing up now, "with all the trials and tribulations ahead."

I don't like that bit, not at all. Stephen has just come *back* from hospital, I've rescued the kids from a fate worse than *death*, for goodness' sake, on that dreadful farm, I've got my ten-pound notes, the boiler's shown it works. We've done the trials and *all* the tribulations.

But I'm in for a penny, I'm in for five pounds. Time to meditate, then: I'll give it a go. It's not my favourite thing at the Manor, I get bored. But, "It's easy," Edwin has said.

He's even given me another tape especially for this: guided meditations to help me along.

"Just focus on your breathing, nice and gentle, nice and deep – listen to the sound of my voice; picture yourself surrounded with the palest violet light – the Violet Flame of St Germain…"

"Wasn't he something to do with the French Revolution?"

Well I do revolutions too. Maybe I'll like this fellow with his violet lights. Who knows? In, out; in, out. I glance at the clock from time to time; I'm not sure I've got time for this. There's the washing to do and – lots of things. There must be; there always are. Close your eyes, girl. In, out; in, out. Is Stephen OK? His French teacher has been so *dumb* since his illness. She doesn't get it at all; he's convalescent, for heaven's sake, and all she goes on about is he missed his exam. He was in *hospital*, see? In, out; in, out. Oh and that lovely violet light – don't forget that. Oh but they're missing the dog, my precious babes. They're missing her so *much*.

I keep on going for two minutes, maybe three. And then I find myself in floods of tears. "I'll give that a miss then."

The off button gets a sharp tap from my index finger.

My teacher's voice vanishes into the silence of the room. Outer silence, that is: inside is chaos. But I can't diss him, this unlikely mentor.

His wisdom takes my breath away and he blazes with a truth that I can't deny. My world-view is changing in spite of me.

14

Light bulb moments

Put a human being into multiple shocks and the organism will cope in all kinds of remarkable ways. Take head injury, for instance. The brain will pour endorphins into the system; they pump up your body and mind like an inflatable cushion, padding your tissues and telling you that everything's just fine.

"We're off to your mother's funeral on Friday," you tell this brain-bashed person.

"Super," she replies.

That's me. I'm not head-injured in the conventional sense; I'm just tipped mildly out of my mind. Kind of not quite sure how much more loss and change I can take. I'm relieved, though, at the same time – and grateful, back in the cottage in the warmth. Stephen is frail but safe. There's a few months' work ahead of us to get him back to health, but time is something we seem to have a little more of than before.

My endorphins are simple ones: they are my cosmic sense of freedom and relief; they're the social security and that lovely, radiator warmth. My cells grin idiotically as I wander to the post office to collect those magical ten-pound notes. It's a temporary mechanism, this endorphin system. Reality will break through, sure as the dawn. With a bit of luck, you'll be adjusting yourself by then. Or else, perhaps, it's beginning to look just a bit more brutal than you thought.

Each new day dawns relentless. As days turn to weeks, I have to summon all the courage I can dig for to crawl from under the covers. The light of day is the last thing I want.

But my new friends at the Manor House have a rather different spin on this question of light. They are of the opinion that light is unreservedly a *good* thing. The entire universe, I'm discovering, is built from this basic resource; light-energy is the secret behind it all. And I learned years ago, like most of us did in school, that when you shine light through a prism, or a raindrop, it breaks out into a whole rainbow of different hues.

I'm invited on a course: a full, six-day event during which all kinds of mysteries will unfold. So I'm here with the students and I'm discovering that there's rather more to this business of colour than red means stop and green means go – though this is true as well. There's more to it, even, than orange is for shock and blue is for peace.

I'm shown that hues and tints and tones are embedded symbolically, ecologically, physically and culturally in all of our races and societies and it's even reflected in the way we think and feel. It's a kind of universal language and it unites everyone around the globe. We're all human; we're all essentially the same. You can be Mongolian or Ethiopian, you can come from the frozen steppes of Alaska or the sweltering sands of the Sahara but you'll still *see red*, you'll still be *yellow-bellied*. On a good day you'll still be *in the pink*.

It will go even further than this, I shall find later. We don't just think the same, feel the same, behave much the same. We're all one swirling energy field, we're all the same stuff.

"No man is island." That's what the poet John Donne said.

This is true; man – and woman too, come to that – is more like *soup*, quantum soup. What seems to be keeping him in place is something we can't see at all: it's consciousness, which produces an idea; the idea then becomes a template, and this template gathers energy into itself and creates form, aka you, me or him.

What's more, we are proactive co-creators in this soup, this ever-moving ocean of pure potential, building our bodies and our *worlds* through the quality and content of our thoughts.

Beam out your message of love or hatred, gratitude or resentment, neediness or plenitude, and the universe will beam it right back at you. Your message will show up as the conditions of

71

your life. Plus, of course, those thoughts are also having quite some effect on other people as well as yourself.

All this takes a bit of believing, need I say. As for me, my Western mind – my body too – says "yeah right." Here in the Manor, though, as I take this class, a lot of my old would-be certainties are being shaken loose.

So here is my teacher, busily explaining that we create our very own reality, every day, just like Edwin suggested on that disturbing tape:

"Quite an interesting idea, I guess..." my head responds silently, as it ponders this thesis a little more. "It doesn't apply to me, of course."

Obviously it doesn't. I'm the victim here, anyone can see that. Life is the thing that happened to me when I was planning something else. There I am, then, inside the safety of my mind, nice and snug. The head's a good place; it's reliable. Stay safe inside it and you can stay outside everything else.

This may not be an option though, not inside these walls: it's my turn for a reading, just like the kind magenta woman proposed the first time I came to visit. There are 20 or 30 people in the room, garnered from all corners of the globe. We're learning a universal language – it's called colour – and we're finding out how it relates to ourselves.

I've chosen an array of those funny little glass bottles, full of glinting oils and herbs: all the tints and combinations that I like best. They remind me of the tropical fish and the orchids and silks and gemstones I saw in Thailand.

All the people around me are looking at these colours that I've chosen from the darkness of my hidden heart and soul, and they're throwing in their observations because the colours, it seems, are an outer reflection of what is going on inside us. They show us who we are, where we've come from, where we're going, and what we need.

These comments come at me like darts, one after another,

relentless and shocking; but they're warm. And they're all about *me*. These simple hues and tones that I've chosen – so innocently, unconsciously – are downloading information straight on to some kind of invisible screen that everyone in the room can see. Except me, of course.

"How can she possibly know that? And that. And that."

I'm alarmed; encouraged; stripped naked; reassured.

"No, it's not navel-gazing," I will explain later to the sceptics. "A narcissist would never dare observe herself with such penetration. She'd be terrified of what she might see. This dismantling of one's self-image is the very opposite of navel-gazing: it has everything to do with self-responsibility; it's about growing up."

I don't know that yet, of course. I haven't a clue about very much at all. I'm Dorothy, lost on Planet Oz. I'm here because I was invited but all I want is to go home.

Well, the teacher's a bit of a wizard, it seems: there's hope for me yet. It's bizarre, though, the way these guys are 'reading' me. They must be psychic, every one of them; they're obviously people who are odd and rare. How did the Old Manor people find them all, and get them over here? I'll never get anywhere near this art that it's been suggested I should try to learn.

"I am not worthy to receive you."

These are the words that I've heard and been required to repeat in my youth, every Sunday of every year. They have translated in daily life, to: "You're not good enough; you'll never make it; don't expect too much. Look after everyone else, though, and hey guess what? You just might get lucky; you may get a small slice of the pie."

This language has been a poison drip, fed straight into my blood. For how long, I wonder? All my life, I guess; but there's a strong suggestion that the cycle has been way longer than that – a suggestion that it goes right back through the mists of time.

"But only say the Word," the liturgy repeats, "and my soul

shall be healed."

Some little ounce of rebellion stirs inside me. It's a whisper, another small voice from the future. Just who is it who must say the Word? And what is the Word, anyway?

"I *am* worthy, dammit! *I am not guilty.*"

I'm in a dream, an altered state of reality. My senses seem to come and go, as though I'm drifting in and out of sleep. They zoom in, these laser beams of insight that people are speaking all around me, to the places in my heart and soul that no-one has ever reached.

Now I'm heaving, dissolving, as the grief and shock and bewilderment of a thousand lifetimes come rushing from the depths. I'm a torrent, a rushing river; but it's a dark tunnel, the place I'm in; there's no light, only anger and sadness and confusion and fear.

The air around me is like black ink; but now there's no energy left for tears. Like a child in kindergarten, tired after a morning's reading, writing and learning to count, I am gently dismissed.

So I swim through this sepia sea to a warm, vacant bed and sleep for the rest of the day. But when at last I wake, the sepia has dispersed. The landscape around me seems to have changed: it's damp and glistening in a light that's fresh and new.

Maybe there's hope for us yet.

15

July 1993

We've made it through another winter, our first season on our own.

The cat left long ago: she simply walked off into the woods and died, merely days after we'd left the farm. The dog has temporarily moved South, to a long-suffering sister.

No no, says Mr Paratrooper, he doesn't have an hour to spend with his children. Most inconvenient. They are not his responsibility now.

He sees them occasionally, on a whim, at moments of his choosing. On these occasions he tells them that it's a bad idea to have children. You even have to house and clothe and feed them; this is what Her Majesty's government has been telling him – the cheek of it. But not to worry, he's working to get himself made redundant, then the problem won't arise. Their mother is wicked, he adds. This is his mantra, repeated like the liturgy itself. They don't believe it, as it happens – not the last line, anyway. It's just possible – at last, at long last – that neither, indeed, do I.

This is a helpful little article I've picked up: think of the worst, *worst* thing that he (or she) does, it says. Think of this person that you're with, in the early stages of your time together when everything is rosy, and the worst thing they ever do in these rosy early days, then fast-forward to the divorce. Now you can multiply that thing by ten million times.

I'm not alone then, in this experience of divorce. I'm more like a statistic of some kind; that's a good thing to know.

My colour training is going nicely now. I'm getting the hang of this interesting new language. Maybe I'll soon start doing some of those 'readings' myself. I can find some clients and they'll even *pay* me to give them this service. We'll climb out of this mess; we can't live on social security for ever.

Yes, there's a rainbow out there. The future's looking as though it might just have a little of that light I've been learning about: not the cold unfeeling sort that points up your world with sharp brutality; more the warm sunny sort that offers solace and renewed hope. It's only a glimmer, perhaps, that I'm seeing, but it's there, unmistakable.

I'm ready to get out into the wide world and start doing my work, whatever form it's meant to take. And I'm looking forward to it: I love my kids, they're my allies and closest friends, but round-the-clock child care without respite or change is not my most natural talent. I like to get out and about. I like working with grown-ups too. After fourteen years of parenting, with all the children now settled in their schools, it feels like the right time to move gently into the next phase. Good. I'm working with a couple of friends to get a little therapy centre going in the local town.

It's Saturday morning. That sun I'm thinking about has just shown up, right outside our window. Magdalen's six now: blonde and beautiful. She's playing with a neighbour. I've just been next door and checked on them, made sure they were doing OK; they're watching a video together, laughing and holding hands. So now I'm back here talking to my sister on the phone.

The little girl comes rushing in, the one that Magdalen's been playing with next door. She's screaming at the top of her voice.

"Magdalen's been run over," she yells.

I go out to the road. My baby is lying there on her face. She heaves quietly a time or two and then she is still.

There's a young woman sitting on the fence of our small garden, screeching and flapping her arms; there's a car stalled beside the hedge. I'm sitting on the road beside my child, a hand gently resting on her back. I'm doing the only thing I know, letting my hand rest there with a vague sense that something, some kind of miraculous life force, might come through and save the day.

I'm not really thinking at all, just breathing and staying still. It seems crystal clear to me that she's dying.

A crowd is gathering. It's only minutes before my teacher from the Manor shows up in his car. He's a wizard, this man. He's already given me untold time and rescue; he's shown me giant steps in how to turn one's life around.

His name is Gabriel: he's a messenger; a channel, a bringer of knowledge. I didn't know there were healers as potent as this anywhere on the planet. He is probably the only person in the cosmos who can bring a whisper of reassurance; a hint that there's some kind of order in this crazy world. The ambulance men have arrived too. They move to interfere with whatever it is that Gabriel is doing.

"Don't touch her!" they tell him. He ignores them and I quietly signal to them to let him be.

"She's going to make it, I'm certain," Gabriel says.

I'm in a neighbour's car. The ambulance has taken Magdalen to the local hospital. She'll soon be transferred at lightning speed to the larger place seventy miles up the road. They'll be banning the rest of the traffic from the mile-long bridge to let the ambulance through. The hospital where we're headed has a brain surgeon who's said to be the best in the country at this mind-bending job. I guess this is miracle number one.

The report is dismal, all the same. I'm there now with my ex-husband, my child's father, as the surgeon emerges. It's most unlikely they can save her life, he says, and if by a whisker they're able do so, the brain damage has already happened. It will only remain to assess the extent of it.

I don't believe him. There's a wizard close by and he's told me something else. There are other angel helpers out there too. I don't know this yet, but my neighbour Judy over the road – someone with not even minimal skills in first aid – reached the scene even before I did and heard a message from some disembodied voice, telling her to rearrange Magdalen's head and tongue so her air passage would be cleared. Ah, so *that* was miracle number one. Judy will get an award for this later on. She deserves it, seven million times over: she has saved my child's life.

I'll hang in there with every ounce of my belief. I won't tell a soul about what's happened, either. I shall not call family or friends, because I'm beginning to understand something quite crucial about the nature of energy. I don't want anything to come near this precious child except the craziest optimism, the most improbable degree of faith. Not a shadow of doubt and fear must undermine the task that we face.

If she's going to do this thing of staying alive she's going to need all the help she can get, all the high-vibration energy the Universe can provide to hold her in a place beyond that of the grim picture she's facing. As long as I can whip myself up to the job, I shall stay beside her. When I can't, I'll give her some space.

The grapevine, of course, has other plans. It starts with the local press and in no time at all the hospital phone is red-hot; it never stops for days. In despair, the nurses beg us half a week later to ask those well-wishers to combine their efforts and condense their messages through fewer channels. But all the people I didn't want in my mind are a life-saver in the flesh. As hours turn into days, steady faith is impossible to hold.

There's something else happening as well, unknown to me as yet. Gabriel is sitting by his phone at home. He's in touch with every student who has ever been near the Old Manor. All over the world, there's a vigil going on around the clock, and Gabriel himself never sleeps for three days and nights. He's been through something pretty much exactly like this himself, five years ago, but worse; he knows this thing from the inside. He's damned if he's going to let it happen again. He couldn't save his own son, with all the help of the Gods: he will save this child if it's the last thing he does.

There are two nurses in charge of Magdalen's care, angels both. They too are working on her around the clock. One of them is constantly by her side. And now, of course, there are healers too –

all kinds, from near and far. They slip in and out quietly, never disturbing what fractured tranquillity we can find in this hushed place where life hangs in the balance. And sleep? I don't do this either; there's not a hope. So I'm lying here, my long-suffering friend Hattie asleep in the bed nearby. This is the companion who first showed up from heaven a few months ago, sharing her house with us fledgling gypsies. Compassion on legs.

But I'm angry now, angry from the pit of my soul. Please sleep on, dear Hattie, no human being can help me here. I'm screaming inside. Don't come near me. I'm savage and wild, and deeply into myself; no-one needs *me* for a friend. I don't like anybody very much, and especially I don't like God. He's the only one I want to speak to all the same.

"God!" I yell silently, from an inner furnace. The quiet is deafening and dark. "Everything – every *last* thing – happens for a reason, that's what they've been telling me. Prove it then. What's this one about? Tell me *that*."

Christ walks in. Now this isn't the stuff of Sunday mornings; it's the real deal: the hair, the face, the robe, the works. Not that I'm impressed, nor even grateful – not the least.

"*You* tell me! Why this? What *for*? Why her? Why *this* child, hardly even out of nursery? What should an innocent six-year-old have to learn? Is it *me*? Am I supposed to be learning something – more, again? Why doesn't it *stop*? Why can't we lead our lives quietly and happily, like everyone else?"

"It's about trust," he says, "You must learn to trust."

"I've heard that one before," I scoff. "I've done it, over and over, right from the inside. There's nothing you can teach me about *that*."

"For her," he continues, "it's something else, a voluntary act of sacrifice: she's doing this for many, many people."

"So will she come back?"

That's all I'm interested in right now. Gabriel has said it; Edwin has said it; William has said it. They've all said she'll make it. But do I dare believe it? Do I dare – even in the privacy and silence of my heart and soul – grab hold of the 'faith – let alone the peace – that passeth understanding' and fly in the face of all the medics' worst predictions?

"She'll come back. And she'll help countless numbers of people in the future."

In the future, I'm thinking... I can't even *see* a future. What about now? Haven't we taken just about enough?

"When's it going to finish," I ask, still screaming, still silent. "When does this cycle stop and make way for something more useful?"

He gazes at me. The eyes are deep pools; lasers of love that beam through to your core and melt it right into themselves. There's nowhere you'd rather be.

"When you've changed," he replies.

I gasp.

"When *I've changed*? And how am I supposed to do that, in the middle of this ongoing nightmare that dares to call itself a life?"

"By learning to trust," he replies.

I'm dumbstruck. The fighting stops, the sobs break out; the torrents are in full flow again. This extraordinary figure comes gently towards me; he sits on my bed and holds my hand. His skin is smooth and olive, his face long, sensitive, finely sculpted. The hair is just like you see in the pictures, flowing, dark and soft. And the hands... I've never seen or felt anything like them anywhere. They're spellbinding: slim and fine and very gentle.

And now he's gone – vanished as quietly and gracefully as he arrived.

But soon dawn breaks again. I creep from the bedroom as the first rays of light come through the curtains; I won't disturb Hattie in her rest. I'm hardly aware of it yet, but something inside has shifted just a fraction. I go through once more to the ITU.

"She's pulling through," the nurses say. "It looks like she's going to make it, after all."

They ask me things about healers and healing. "What is it you've all been doing?" they ask. "Where can we learn about all this ourselves?"

Because, they say, the impossible has happened and they don't understand.

I look at them with gratitude, admiration, awe. As far as I'm concerned, they're the miracle-workers.

I'm rejoicing in their wonderment and shining faces. And I'm quiet now, as I wonder what possessed me to give my child this birth name.

She's never liked it, always said she'll take up another name – something more *normal*, for heaven's sake.

Magdalen was Jesus Christ's best friend.

16

Thoughts on science

The Dalai Lama keeps up to date with the latest scientific discoveries and has a special interest in what's happening in the world of quantum physics. He always says that if it ever came to a conflict between science and religion, he would tend to go with science. In fact, he encourages us to throw out even the words of the Buddha himself if science proves them wrong.

What's been happening in that intensive care unit is not religion.

My conflict with religion is finished anyway, the last of that battle-torn relationship with my birth-dogma washed out last year along with the bathwater of my marriage. If religion means church, it's over.

No, this is not religion; it's something else. It does involve communication with the unseen, of course, and religion through the centuries has clearly involved itself with that.

The thing that is being created in this unit is a miraculous interface between the realms of spirit and science. Without the aid of the medics, my child would probably not have lasted more than an hour or two beyond the crash. Without the aid of spirit, who can ever say?

"Keep talking to her," Gabriel has told me earlier, as we set off to follow the ambulance. "And remind her that you love her. That will make all the difference."

So here I am on that very first day, after the first of her brain surgeries, and I'm holding Magdalen's bandaged head. She is deeply unconscious. The task of breathing and all the other jobs a body must do have been taken on by the machines around her. I'm talking to her about the party we shall have when she's better; about her bedroom at home. I'm telling her that when she's well

82

again I'll paint her room pink. And yes, I love her, way more than my life: have I ever shown her that enough?

"She likes that," says our friend, a near-neighbour who's sitting at her feet. "Keep on talking. She likes the bedroom, the party – specially the party."

"Has he gone psychic too?" I wonder, bemused. That seems to be the way of the world these days. It's simpler than that: he's reading the brain monitor. It keeps shooting up near to danger levels. But talk of pink walls, love, balloons, and it comes back down again. Keep on talking and it stays there.

These are a few of my favourite things.

This interface between the seen and the unseen worlds is borne out by more than the surgery and the hi-tech. It's being lived, moment to moment, in the quiet harmony of nursing staff and healers, each offering the other such gratitude and deep respect.

What is happening here in the realm of spirit cannot be quantified or measured; there's no control group and I'm no scientist. I've nothing to go on except the few observations I'm making – but there are some remarkable things to observe. That first night took us into the deepest crisis. In a last-ditch attempt to save her, they operated for a second time. I was sent away to rest for an hour or two but there was soon an emergency call to my room.

"You'd better come at once."

I'm shell-shocked and dim, but there's no mistaking what they mean. My request from the moment of impact has been simple and I've sent it to God. Use me if you can, in any way you can, as a conduit for whatever life force she can handle, but not an ounce more. For a moment or two I have been frightened of bringing my *self* in here, overdoing the charge out of fear, but it doesn't last. I know the process has nothing to do with me.

I know something else as well: in any healing, it's the client, the other person, who is doing it, not the so-called healer. This other person can support the process, for sure, but the decision to draw any energy through, to grow and change in any way at all, to *heal*, comes from the person receiving that energy – even if the person seems to be as deeply unconscious as a human being can be. So I've sent my request to Magdalen as well. I have been laying my hands on her – on and off – ever since she emerged from the operating theatre the first time, but all has been still; not a whisper of a breeze has passed through my arms or my hands.

And now we're on her last chance: I'd call it the moment of choice. It's 3 am – the dead of night; my hands are resting on her battered head. All of a sudden, I feel a rush of energy move through my whole body. I've worked with my hands for years, in a simple way for healing, but I've never felt a sensation like this.

What I don't know is that back in the village, seventy miles away, others are active too. Judy, the neighbour who first kept Magdalen breathing, has just awoken. She's meditating in her garden, and in the light that she's drawn in she is quietly holding an image of this child fully healed, whole.

Even Magdalen's father back at the farm, Mr Outward Bound himself, has just woken too. Gabriel, of course, has never even tried to sleep. He's staying tuned to the whole event, from one moment to the next. He will tell me later that Magdalen 'died' twice – once on the road, once now, at three o'clock that night – but this second time is the moment she's decided that whatever it takes to do it, she will come back, and she will stay.

Some days later, before we know the decision that Magdalen apparently took in the small hours of that first night, Hattie makes friends with the hospital chaplain.

"I don't usually see things like this," he says, "or say them – but I've been seeing pictures in my mind's eye: clear pictures of Magdalen as a teenager."

A week later, my child is off the machines and I am allowed to hold her in my lap. For just a few seconds she wakes; there's a smile on her face as she gazes straight into my eyes.

"Mummy," she says. "Party. Pink curtains. Ice cream."

But those are precisely the things I've been talking to her about as she lay unconscious!

"Who's in charge around here?" I wonder. "Who's running the show?"

Some days later, she comes to again. This time, her eyes are seeking and searching. They're scanning the room.

"Wispa," she murmurs.

Ah. This is a much harder request to meet.

I've promised her a swimming trip with the dolphins, though, as soon as I can bring it about. It's what she's always wanted and she's specially going to need it now. She's obviously heard this piece, too. I have every intention of keeping my promise, of course I have. How on earth am I going to do it, and when?

Let's not think about that right now. Let's focus on one small step at a time. Just for the moment, there's only one job we have to do: get this precious child out of that hospital bed; get her on her feet; get back home.

Another couple of weeks and her walking lessons will begin.

A journey of a thousand miles begins with a single step.

It's a much-quoted nugget of wisdom offered centuries ago by Lao-Tzu, and never has it been more true.

17

Back home

My baby has been rescued from the jaws of death and we've been back in the cottage for a few weeks. The drama's finished, everyone's gone away on their summer breaks, soaking up the sea and sun. Even the local paper has finished running the story: the world has turned the page as it's moved on to its next chapter, and the house is silent as a chapel.

I know, deep in my bones, that our journey has only just begun. I remember to send out words of gratitude every hour of every day.

I marvel constantly and gratefully at the gift of my child, delivered back to my arms against all the odds – I'll give myself that. But the silt that was already sitting in my veins when I squatted in my church hideout has leaked right through and taken up permanent residence in my heart. I'm in black despair and I can't see beyond the end of my nose.

Magdalen will learn to walk again. She'll come to feed herself too. Her flowing blonde locks are a thing of the past as she crawls from room to room, bemused, her head semi-shaven, bruised, sawn and scarred.

There's a ton of clothes for her to choose from – I got them from a market stall, every colour in the wildest bed of flowers. There's only one set she will wear, though: pink leggings, purple shirt. She spills her food all over them and looks panic-stricken if you ask her to wear anything else. I wash them every night so they're dry in the morning.

The words are coming back – just a few, struggling and hesitant. She calls her sister Robert. For me, she has no name at all.

I'll thank you in my heart, years later, for your visits, your phone calls, the whirlwind of energy that sustained us through the inferno; but I doubt I'm remembering to do this now. The world must look after me, it's obvious; I can't do this alone. And if it's hell we've just escaped from, it's nowhere-land that we're shacked up in now.

I don't know where we've been or where we're going. There is no path, no future, no way out. If we try very very hard, we can just about make it through one day at a time.

My social and emotional boundaries are growing blurred; I'm forgetting how life in the regular world is done. What's yours and what's mine? I hardly know the difference. Give me what you have; I'll take it all.

Death would be sweet but I have to survive. Give me all the time you have and then some. I'll talk at you, through you. I'm myopic, needy and dull. Stay with me. I cannot do this alone.

No, I'll think again: don't come near me if you value your life. I'll be angry with you, or worse; I'll bore holes right through you, through your very soul. My heart is dessicated and stiff.

But I'm Dorothy and lest I forget it, I have three friends. If my heart is feeling old and dry, theirs are young and warm. Magdalen's small body may be crawling along the floor, but her soul is shining bright. She looks on as I show some hospital photographs to a visiting friend. I'm not alarmed to let my child see the images of this new and different person: tell her gently that she's had an accident and her face breaks into a grin. It's obvious that she has little idea of what's been going on. Besides, I've not strayed more than a few yards from her since the start, and I've made sure she'll never see a mirror. The photos won't touch her at all. She crawls over to us and clambers on to my knee.

"That's me; that's me; that's me," she says, pointing to the little girl in the photographs – the one with the drips and wires, the bandages and the broken head. Then another photo comes out: I've snapped the camera towards her a few weeks earlier as she's ridden a pony on the beach, blonde hair flowing in the wind. It was on the same reel: a bizarre set of before-and-after images that all arrived by the same post – to taunt us, or to offer us hope?

"Who's that?" she asks.

Her face has that bewildered look again, as she peers at the child we all knew a month or so before. For herself, it seems, she has no recognition at all. But with that battered creature in the hospital, the one her eyes have never seen in any looking-glass, she's currently all at home.

Make of that what you will. We have eyes and ears and tongues, but we have other perceptions too. Who knows how small are the senses we know, in the bowl of this vast universe? Who knows what is really going on when we believe someone is unconscious or asleep?

I take her to the market, to find the high-potency foods she needs to rebuild her shrunken frame. I needn't worry about what to choose, she does it for me. From the seat of her pushchair, she points to everything she needs: bright green pea pods, deep green leaves, sunshine peppers, berries in burgundy, scarlet and rose.

Edwin calls, asks how we're getting on. "She'll be keenly in touch with her higher self at the moment," he says, "tuned into all the things she needs – especially the colours. Let her show you the way."

It seems that this is what she's doing already. She can't speak, except for the occasional word, but her colour-messages are clear enough.

So we lurch along from one day to the next, tackling each hour, each day, with whatever equanimity we can find. Sleep is a thing of the past: I must stay alert, because this six-year-old can climb over the rails of her cot and open the door; she could easily tumble down the steep flight of stairs and bash that precious head some more.

So one early morning I'm out of the room for half a minute too long and she does exactly that: she climbs out of her cot, but she opens a different door from the one I've feared. It gives access to a cupboard that has a full-length mirror inside. She's bumping her way down the stairs now, screaming as she goes. She has remembered my name lately and now she's hitting me with everything she has – her fists, her feet, her eyes.

"Why did you cut my hair off?" she blazes. "Why? *Why*?"

For fourteen years to come, that sight of herself in the mirror will be the earliest memory she has.

I bundle her into the car, hugging her, kissing her for dear life. We're both in floods of tears. I drive to the local town and we search the shops. We shall find the *most* beautiful hat that ever was made. She finds it for herself – blue denim – pulls it on her head and never takes it off for the next two years.

I had a child who was vibrant and joyful, active and alert. Life was a wonderful adventure to her and she relished every moment. Not any more: she's hardly back in her body; she's way out, somewhere in space.

As the weeks turn to months, she will move a little further back in, she'll become a little more present, but she's lost her life force and the wish to live: in order to come back into physical life at all, she has drawn on the deepest energy reserves of her soul: she's used them all up. But now she has to do life and this is a different thing entirely. She has a body to rebuild, battered connections in her brain to re-wire. The basic skills for living will have to be learned over again from scratch. How to do this, when she's running on empty?

She will sit on a sofa and watch her movies. Later, she will play a little with her dolls and even with the coloured bottles.

She doesn't want to move though. You can suggest a walk but no thanks - she doesn't like the outside world. She can't balance to ride a bike, her co-ordination is gone, so the music she loved so much is closed. She can listen, but not play. Besides, there's nothing that makes her want to sing: her spirit is broken, just like mine. We're together, the blind leading the deaf.

The months are going by, the seasons change. It's time for a holiday: I must sell the rest of my books. Let's swap them for high-vitality food. We'll have strawberries and put cream on top. We'll go fetch some of that stuff that memories are made of – the good ones. A theme park is the thing. I book a B&B for two nights and watch as the children whoop and whirl. She's only allowed on the gentlest of rides. But I'm watching her: little by little, this child is coming back to life. And as I watch, an outrageous idea arrives in my mind like a balloon from some other-worldly cartoon.

"We can change the past," says the idea.

It's ludicrous, of course. Logically, it's outrageous and impossible. The past is in my face, every moment of the day. It's in *her* face, her body, her battered skull. It haunts me in my dreams. It bars me, like a torturer, from sleep. But the voice goes on.

"We can eradicate what we no longer need. We shall reach a place in the future where the accident never happened," it insists. Quiet but firm.

"She's finally gone mad," my aunt has commented to one of my sisters a few months before, as she has kept up with the hospital news from the safety of her home in the South. She was referring to me, of course. She has heard about the healers, the psychics. She knows I've been avoiding the statutory hysteria of the situation as I've asked for tranquillity and calm.

If this is madness, I think, as this new possibility courses through my veins and nerves, then there is method within it somewhere.

Maybe the rest of the world could use a little of this madness too. I shall tell no-one about it, not a solitary soul, but I shall hold it in front of me. I shall hold the vision, keep the faith. My child will be healed, one hundred per cent. And I shall search the universe until that vision comes to pass.

Another winter has passed; a fresh year is breaking into life. There'll be a long, long way to go on this thousand-mile trek, this strange human journey that's so full of hazards and solace, dangers and rewards.

My child's journey, your journey, my journey; his, hers, theirs: the details vary a little, but really it's all the same.

We're God in human form, divine sparks coming to know themselves better through the journey of life on Planet Earth.

We're meeting ourselves through the often disconcerting medium of contrast: finding who and what we are by learning all that we are not.

We experience separation, sometimes in the most extreme ways, so that one day, each of those God-sparks comes to rediscover its true nature and returns to oneness.

But I don't know this yet. I don't know that we are all part of one another, that what happens to one of us at some level touches us all.

I'm alone and fighting. I'm fighting off the despair that comes at me in waves, threatening to engulf me and drown us all. But through it all, I hold to this one, preposterous idea: my child will be fully healed, one hundred per cent.

Comment

Eternal Covenant

"Have you ever had toothache?" the master asks.

"Yes," his student replies.

"And do you remember how it felt?" the master continues.

"Yes," the boy replies again.

"Were you able to think about anything else?"

"No," says the boy.

And that, the master explains, is the human condition: most people suffer from spiritual toothache. He's Tony de Mello, this teacher, a Catholic priest. I love his work, not least because he's a rebel. He debunks his own religion and gives people back to themselves.

So that would be it then. My disease has a name – I can get a handle on it now. I could give it another name, of course; I could call it pathological self-absorption. But no, I prefer de Mello's terminology. Spiritual toothache has a clearer ring to it; it offers hope. You can fix a toothache, after all; one day it will go away.

Everything is fluid; all is change; nothing lasts – not even the nightmares. Eight months after my "soul reading", in the aftermath of the smash, Edwin is one of the first people who has told us that we're not to worry, Magdalen will survive. He's also told us that, just for the moment, her aura looks like a stained glass window that has been shattered and stirred in a glass of water.

It's an image that makes sense. That's how it feels – all of it. Life, home, children, cash, contentment, peace, safety. You name it, it's smashed.

But when my sister, who visited us in hospital every day with parcels of food, suggested that I rub Magdalen's skin with a rainbow of colours in chakra order, it felt like a good idea:

something like those films where you play it backwards, so that water flows back through the taps or a person walks backwards up a flight of stairs. Perhaps we can reverse the movie, put this precious Humpty-Dumpty child of mine back together again – and the rest of us too, come to that.

Because if those ancient acupuncturists are anywhere near the mark, if there's any truth in this notion that the light body comes first and the dense body follows on from it, well *this* little light body could sure do with some extra help in re-arranging itself.

So we'll fast-forward here a little, we'll wind the reel *onward* to where we might be at some time in the future, as the reality of angelic healing really comes to ground and life begins to make some kind of sense again.

I understand none of this yet; its usefulness has not impacted yet on our new, nightmare reality, but one day I shall see that we're not really our dense bodies after all; these are merely the temporary forms we take up in order to make our earthly journeys. And I shall discover that true healing has a lot to do with reconnecting with our true nature – which is of light.

Here's a short piece of theory, then, that relates directly to the work we did with this broken child, putting her back together again. It's not essential to the story, but it could be useful if you're the kind of person, like me, who likes to know the whys and the hows, and moreover, it begins to make a little sense of the miraculous healing that lies ahead.

If you didn't know this already, then, the chakras are revolving energy wheels, which are arranged within our subtle bodies or our auras: they draw in the universal life force, or light-force, from the field around us, so that this becomes available to the physical body to use.

According to ancient mystics, and more recently backed up by Kirlian and other energy-photographers, each of these centres is also pretty much related to a particular spectral hue.

It's as if these water-based bodies of ours behave something like that droplet of water in the sky on a sunny day: hit them with a beam of light and they break it up into God's own light show, the one he showed Noah when those other waters had finally drained away, a multi-coloured flag or promise of everlasting unity. It's the eternal covenant between the light and the dark.

In perfect health, then, perfect balance that's mental and emotional as well as physical, and with eyes wired up to perceive higher frequencies of light than we generally do at present, we would all look like beautiful rainbows – upside down, perhaps, as red is at the bottom, around our hips and legs and feet, and violet at the top, around the crown of our heads – but if we only had the eyes to see it, we'd be a pretty sight nonetheless.

We don't have eyes to see it, of course, or most of us don't; our physical senses are calibrated to perceive much denser levels than these. And we aren't a perfect rainbow vision, of course; we're human beings, dealing with every kind of pressure for most of the time, and perfect balance and harmony isn't something that many of us know a whole lot about.

The template is there for this to happen, though, and we come close enough to some kind of symmetrical arrangement to know that there's a method here, there's an ideal that's not completely unrealistic. This chakra system is part of the basis for the various systems of colour healing that have come and gone from the planet for a few thousand years.

So this is interesting, maybe, especially if you're concerned to know how to harness light for health, wealth, good companionship or any other state of life you may be seeking.

But the thing that's more pertinent to the task I'm involved in here – which is one of attempting to take some of my own experience and share a little of what useful information I've gleaned along the way – is an observation that Rudolf Steiner, the visionary and philosopher, made in his early twentieth-century teachings. He said that colour itself arises at the interface between darkness and light. Colour is magically born when you take a beam of light and shine it into a dark place.

Now this observation, it seems, can return our focus to the promise that comes from the most ancient of all Biblical mythology, God's promise to Noah, as He placed that arc of colour in the sky after the devastation of the flood. Divinity would re-enter our humanity, He promised, and we wouldn't find ourselves abandoned ever again. Maybe we could climb on board that rainbow and go right back home.

Colour forms a bridge, this is the point. I'm daring to suggest that its role as this connecting link is really quite significant. The implication of all this, surely, is that this light-bridge unites all kinds of things.

Colour is the rainbow arc that comes from God himself; that's the Bible's version of the thing. But those five early books of the Old Testament, the Torah in Hebrew tradition, have been explained by the book of the Zohar, a much earlier source, springing from the oral tradition handed down through thousands of years before any of it was written down.

According to this more ancient mythology, those early ancestors of ours knew that these biblical myths grew out of much more primeval knowledge – they contain coded wisdom which enables us to tap into the power of the universe itself. And that, of course, includes us.

We can glimpse something going on behind the surface of those pretty bright lights, then, that we like to surround ourselves with: the colours that we choose to eat or drink or wear. In this mysterious universe where the energy of light lowers its vibration to become the physical world that we know, ultimately all that we experience, every physical form, is born of light itself. As light turns into something that we know as material substance, what is really happening is that it's becoming denser. And if it's becoming denser it's becoming darker. Colour is the bridge, then, between spirit and matter. It balances the two.

Colour is also the interface between the day and the night, and the implication of this is profound: colour must in fact be the stepping stone between the divided parts of ourselves, those aspects of our nature that we embrace in light and warmth, and those that we suppress in shadow; the parts of us, in other words, that we accept, and those that we deny.

If there's something out there that we have called God, then this something most certainly lives inside us too. And if there's something in us that is called the ego, there is a much greater part of us that is called the soul.

And colour, somehow or other, can help us bring all this together.

It can help us reconnect the scattered parts of ourselves; it can jog our memories so that we reclaim the pieces of ourselves that we've given away.

It can even help us make that trek from the barren land of ego, where frustration is the order of the day, to the fertile ground of the heart and soul – that great expansive place where things warm up a whole lot.

Now that is a pledge worth pursuing.

Three

The albatross will fly up to five thousand miles
in order to fetch squid for its young

18

Spring 1994

Nine months have passed since we returned from the hospital to the cottage, and some small semblance of order is creeping back into our lives. Magdalen is not back in school full-time yet, but her hours are slowly growing.

Activities at the Manor House are expanding apace, too, as a growing body of students filters in from further and further afield. I've been through all the courses, I'm certificated, and my mentor has just asked me to do something; but it's ridiculous.

"I can't," I say.

"Yes you can," says Gabriel. "Just do it."

He's asking me to teach a foundation course in colour therapy to a group of students, in my front room. He obviously doesn't get it at all: there's no *way* I can teach.

"I don't even understand the stuff," I tell him.

"Yes you do. It's all there inside you. You know it; you've known it for aeons."

"What about the children?"

"You can fit the schedule around their school day."

What's to stop me? It's not my teacher posing the question, of course, it's me. He's fast-tracked me expressly for this purpose. Am I really going to refuse the chance to break out, to break us *all* out? I don't believe I can do it, but there are times when we need a Wizard, someone who spots what we've missed in ourselves – like the one in Oz, for instance. He knows that Dorothy can do life as well as anyone: she just needs a reminder.

"Here's a medal to prove it," Oz tells her, when she's emerged after her tussles with the Wicked Witch – and what's the Wicked Witch if it's not the ego? And what's the ego if it's not the part of us that wants to stop us growing; to keep us safe and small?

"Here, take it," he continues. "Hang it round your neck. And while you're at it, give some encouragement to your friends: medals, certificates, whatever you like. They're great guys, those chums of yours – wisdom, love and courage."

Dorothy's friends are her friends, of course, but they're also reflections of what she holds inside – just like our own friends who stand as mirrors before us, showing us some of our shadow and much of our light. As her friends are gathering up brass badges and testimonials and what-not for all their sterling qualities, perhaps she'll start believing in some of her own. Maybe I will too; maybe I'll find I can do the job after all.

So I do, and the work is not beyond me in the end. It even turns out to be fun. There's life coming in as we fill the house with people and a rainbow array of bottles. We're translating the colour choices these people make into a coherent picture and I'm telling them that energy follows thought. It's something Gabriel has taught us; I'm still not at all sure that I believe a word of it but I'm saying it anyway. Make the commitment to something, the theory goes, and the means to bring the thing about, whatever it is, will follow.

We teach what we need to learn – that's a phrase I seem to keep hearing; and here I am, spilling out my borrowed wisdom: I'm learning fast. We're not halfway through the week before the phone rings:

"Will you come to Canada?" says a voice. "I'm looking for a teacher. They said you might be free."

It's impossible, of course, and I explain why; there are two children involved, sometimes three. I haven't a bean for travelling and there'd be no-one to care for the children if I were to go away. But that's OK, it seems: she'll be sending air tickets for the lot of us. I'll earn enough there, apparently, to pay her back. No, she's not trained yet to teach; she's fascinated by this thing and longing to learn. She will arrange for the children to attend the local school. And Nicola, school holidays? – of course, no problem at all.

What on earth am I supposed to do with this? Stephen is a borderline case already, in the eyes of his teachers. He's an expert in the art of trouser-slashing, he dyes his flowing locks bright pink and sees homework as an optional extra for other people. He's just turned twelve and he's told me last week that he's decided to pass on the grass from now on. He started a local enterprise with a fellow biker, cleaning the neighbourhood cars: so *that's* what he's been doing with the cash. Where does he find dope, I've asked him, and however much does it cost? I don't even know what the stuff looks like.

"Oh no," he says, "I don't have to buy it. It's Andy's Mum and Dad – they grow it in their back garden."

"So that's why they call it weed." You learn something every day.

"I buy my cigarettes, though," he adds. "But I'm giving those up too."

I must have lost my sense of smell.

Maybe Canada's the answer, I muse, as I hang up the phone and start some rapid thinking. There'll be merry hell to pay at school for such gung-ho flouting of the rules, but what do they know, those people who put grammar and syntax before a child's life? And do we really have a lot of choice? Here's another chance to step out of poverty that's corroding our bones. If I refuse the offer of another arm up the ladder, the one that leads back into the world, what then? Maybe I can stack shelves at the Co-op: they pay three pounds twenty an hour.

But this – a trip to the wilds of the North American continent – it's called work experience. Let's do it, kids – let's learn to fly!

"An aeroplane?" says Magdalen. "Jessica went in an aeroplane for her holidays. Will it be like that?"

"Kind of," I reply. "A bit cooler when we get there, perhaps."

I've hit on the Arctic again, of course. We step out of the plane and gasp as the frost slices through our cheeks. I just can't seem to resist that gnawing, bone-shattering freeze: I draw it towards myself like wasps to the jam. The ice on the rivers is six foot thick and skating is the order of the day. So we're shivering but it's sparkling and shiny and new; there's adventure here for all of us.

There will be teaching in Ontario, clients to see in the city, Indian settlements to visit further North. Stephen is enchanted by the medicine stones and dream-catchers, the head-dresses and boots of ancient chiefs.

"He was a Shaman in his last life," says our hostess. "I've felt it in his energy since the moment he arrived."

"Ah yes of course." That was easy.

The kids are exploring the forests and lakes in the Eastern wilds of this untamed land, coming face to face with turtles and mountain bears. If we ever return to those far-off sticks in England, I'll have some chats with his teachers and tell them he's been getting educated. As for me, it's time for work. I leave the children for a couple of weeks as I fly West to teach in Calgary.

First stop Banff. The whole place, all the Rockies, has to be among the Seven Wonders of the World: Redwood forests to take your breath away; trees that soar like heavenly monuments to the azure heights above; hot springs gushing into pools on the mountain side. We climb in up to our necks and feast on the panorama that stretches for miles across the lush greenery and the still blue waters of the lake.

There's quite a group of students to come on this new course, but first, will I please talk about colour healing on a local TV show? I do so quite willingly, and now here's a thing:

They know nothing of my history, those people out there. Not a soul among them knows that my heart is a bleeding, battered steak. They simply see the colours, hear about the colours, and they call the program number, asking for a consultation please. Will I do 60 sessions, the TV producer asks, as she hangs up the receiver yet again? Not possible, but I'll squeeze in 40. And of those 40, I discover as the week unfolds, not less than half have lost a child or nearly lost a child or have a child who's dreadfully sick.

They are Humpty Dumpties, in pieces all. They come with broken lives and hearts, because some part of them has seen the possibilities hidden within light and they're setting out bravely to re-gather their scattered parts.

I'm getting more glimpses here of how the Universe works, and I'll be seeing it time and again, this linking of souls to honour our assignments with people we think we don't know from Adam. It feels like the whole thing has been set up by a higher force before we ever lift a finger or speak a word. Maybe it has.

The weeks fly by swiftly, though, and now we're back in London, at the start of spring: it's warm and fresh and clear. An old friend has come to meet us. I've not seen her in some time.

"So what's the thing with these colours of yours?" she asks.

"They show you what you've wanted to do all the way along," I reply, "and they give you permission to do it.

"They bring the best friends you've never met right into the middle of your life. They remind you that you're the boss – in *your* life anyway. And hey, you know what? They set you free."

19

Summer 1994

But now, reality is bumping towards us fast. A few short weeks back home and we find that our warm respite, our two whole years of central heating, have come to a sudden end. The cottage has been sold and we have a few weeks to find another place. I'm only immovable on two counts: (i) three bedrooms, (ii) a safe garden for a child who's half-absent, totally unsafe anywhere within shouting distance of a road. Fences please: not negotiable.

It's down to the letting agent, then, fast. I tell him our meagre requirements. Do they have something, anything, that meets these criteria? And warm, of course, is always good.

"No, I'm afraid not," says the first one. "Nothing at present."

"I don't believe we have," says the next agent. "No, there's not been much on our books these last few months."

"Nothing of that description," says the third.

"Ah but we have two flats," says the fourth. "This one's above the chemist's; a little small, perhaps. Here's the one above the building society. It has a second bedroom."

The story repeats itself over a radius of sixteen miles. So that's how we end up in Thatched House: well it *used* to be thatched. That was before those now-famous northern gales wore down the resistance of this once-snug roof. Its nice straw padding has – how shall we say it? – lost weight, and from now on the elements will win the battle every time. None of this is evident on a sunny day in August: a picturesque little lane, cute church, rolling meadows. Sheep may safely graze; perhaps we can too.

In your dreams.

But there's nothing else available, not for miles and miles. So here we are, as summer turns to autumn. It's November and the washing up liquid's *frozen*, I tell you, *frozen*. Oh and the streams run down the *inside* of the walls, ceiling to floor – no shortage of water here at least. You've not met the mice of course, but you will, you will. They think they own the place, you see, like something out of Beatrix Potter: Mr Johnny Town Mouse is here with all his friends and relations.

Except that we're living the rural idyll these days. Well, Johnny Country Mouse, then – they're all as arrogant as each other anyway. They stop and stare at you as they scamper across the floor. "Who are you?" they say. "Spending a day in the country? Oh well, make yourself at home, then, do. We've left you some cheese."

"And the kitchen?" I asked the young agent boy back in the summer, the one who was showing us round. He looked a little awkward.

"Where is the kitchen?" I repeat.

"There isn't a kitchen, um, *as such*," he replied, his face faintly apologetic. "The room at the back has a sink. There's a space here; you could put a cooker in if you like."

He's kind, this Saturday boy, you can see it in his face. He really wants us to be happy. He looks around, his face searching for clues. "There's a larder," he adds. "Very characterful, very characterful."

So we take a look at the larder. At a rough guess I'd say it was built by Henry VIII – probably for one of his wives. It's a kind of torture chamber: open the door a half-inch and the temperature drops ten degrees; ten degrees *more*, I mean.

It's far more expensive than the last one, this place: half as much all over again. I could stack shelves at the Co-op right around the clock and never pay the rent, if I had the available time, of course, which I haven't. I have more like four hours a day. Thank God for HM Government. Not that we've got enough left over for logs or anything, which is unfortunate because your teeth start chattering *before* you get out of bed in the morning. So I resort to the only available solution: fetch the children home from school

and we all go to bed, every day. Frozen, like the Fairy liquid,
November to March.

"Hi kids – read any good books lately?"

Salmonby Grange, with its dried-up well and never-ending
winds, was frozen and parched. This place is frozen and
drenched. Just to survive the winter in this sad, sodden hovel
from one day to the next takes all the life-force I can muster. We
pile out of the house for the school run, a dog – floppy-eared and
droopy-jawed – ambles slowly past the door: its owner looks
pretty much the same.

"I should think anyone could be happy if they live in a
thatched house," she remarks, miserably.

"Oh, absolutely," I reply as she walks on up the lane.

There are a few more sad faces around this village. Perhaps it's
the churchyard: all those dead bodies wandering around at night.
They do seem to have a taste for our bathroom; those chills you
get when you're drying yourself have got to be supernatural.

But a small miracle is on its way. Though I say it myself, it's all
because we up-sticksed and flew to Canada. I'm not quite
completely a persona non grata any more. I can flap my wings a
bit. Dammit, I've been on TV! I have to answer the phone again.
It's Gabriel from the Manor House, and he has a question.

"Will you teach the floaty people?"

You bet I will! That would be way more fun than stacking
shelves at the Co-op. He's offering me a salary too, this wizard. A
salary! God bless him, for ever and ever. Goodbye social security,
for ever and ever: it was nice knowing you; thanks for keeping us
alive.

The job is part-time, of course – it depends upon the flow of
people prepared to fly from all corners of the globe to this
unlikely location in the middle of nowhere. But we can buy some
logs. And mouse poison. And several more layers of blankets –
they keep away the frostbite at night. It's a Good Life.

I'll be glad when spring comes though. And then, as if by

magic, that's just what it does: it comes creeping over the window-sill, just like the ones in the poems. With it come the daffodils, right outside our doorstep. And on that lawn, that safe lawn for which we would willingly sacrifice our fingers and toes, come primroses, crocuses, apple blossom... It's a sight to behold.

20

On anger

Anger is a very untamed state of mind, very rough and uneven.
This is what the Dalai Lama has said.

He's right, of course. Anger changes our physiology. Our faces
lose their beauty, they go red and wrinkled, which makes you
wonder what anger is doing to us inside. Sending up our blood
pressure, that's for sure; squeezing our cells, stiffening our joints.
Premature ageing – I'd bet on it. We're all full of it, though, one
way or another. Just take a look at the soap operas. Anger is
something to hold on to when the world feels like it's out of
control.

So I'm doing my job quite nicely. It's just some weeks that the
courses are running. I go on... make breakfast, do the school
round, teach love and light ("You're so serene," they say "where
do you get such wonderful peace of mind?") and on... chop
wood carry water – you know the kind of thing. Oh and pay the
rent.

Ah, that again. There's the rub and it's getting boring. It's not
that I mind that we have to pay for the roof over our heads; it's
just that there aren't any jobs around here to make it possible. I've
probably got the only one that goes an inch or two more than
halfway.

We're stuck in a prison with no visible means of escape,
because we're well into our third year now since our farming
days and behind those brave faces of my two older children
there's an ever-revolving question:

"Any chance of a ride home? Like staying there kind of
home?"

I know that there isn't – not one that I can see in my wildest
dreams. And I'm angry; angry with the world, angry with the

helplessness of it all; angry with me. I cannot abide the fact that I'm doing this to my children and I'm contorted with guilt. Anger's not all bad, mind. It drives you to movement.

The books have gone already, all those novels and poems and plays, long since swapped for a few decent meals: they perked up our diets no end. The jewels went after them, and the dining table, chairs, trinkets and bits all followed. They bought us a holiday: two whole weeks in the sun. *That's* the stuff memories are made of – the ones you like to keep. What next, though? I have nothing left to sell.

If I believe even some of the words I hear myself speak, as I teach those starry-eyed students of colour and light, there's only one solution: I'll have to go inside, a little further into this place of solitary confinement, and see what I can find.

Which means that first I must deal with the anger that's seething inside me, though I'm hardly conscious enough to know that it's there, running me from its place in the dark. And if I even feel it, how do I begin to locate it or define it? What do I do about it? Maybe all I need to do is acknowledge it, at first. Maybe, like all of us, it needs some space: perhaps it wants to be understood.

The child we knew left home the day she was hit. The one who's replaced her is only half-there. Is that the big number, the insurmountable grief, the only one that really matters? The home we knew has gone for ever – where does *this* belong on the scale of my rage? The freedom we thought we had was nothing but an illusion. The father my kids thought they had has evaporated.

Those spurs to fury are just for starters: there's plenty more where they came from. The rage is swirling and thickening. It clenches my muscles and dulls my brain. And it's doing something to my eyes and ears. If this is the stuff that makes the shadow, I don't like it very much at all.

"You've got no sense of humour," says my son. "You never laugh."

Oh my God, he's right. Where did that go? Well, the world just ran right out of things to laugh about – and I'm not joking. That was a rare moment of truth, though. Most of the time, he's busy making it all right for the rest of us. What's he doing with *his* anger? Where can he put that?

They used to see all kinds of fun stuff, those eyes, though if I'm truthful that was probably long ago. It was in a previous life, an age of comfortable and unconscious innocence.

The young eyes saw the beauty and the purity and the hope. The sensory organs revelled in this thing we call life; they leapt up and out to meet the spring; they loved all of the people all of the time. Now my eyes have swapped their lenses: they're seeing the bad stuff – only the bad stuff. And the ears, the ones that heard the joy and all the jokes? Not as sharp as they were, that's for sure. This must be the darkness that Edwin was talking about.

It's universal, of course.

"He's so mean to me; she's a proper bitch. Nobody gets it, nobody cares. I don't *believe* what he just did. I'll get him for this – you see if I don't. This was the *worst* possible thing."

Yes, see me. Watch me, be amazed by me, see how bad I'm feeling, because then I'll know I'm real. You have to validate me, right? You have to climb in there with me, you have to agree that my story is the worst, the very worst – because then I'll know that I'm not only real, maybe I'm even a bit important. Maybe I *matter*.

"My car broke down, right on the motorway; it was *terrible*," you may say, "not a café or a service station for miles."

"Oh I *know*," says your friend, "that happened to me last month, worse: raging hale storm and no reception anywhere."

We're attached to the thick squelchy emotions that come along with a rush of anger, or frustration, or swirling resentment. We love the way they pump us up, make us a bit *more than*: unluckier than you, smarter than her. We love all that energy, all that power. There's not quite enough of it, though. I want more! You just listen to my story then I can maybe have a little of your energy too. Just to get you to hear me is enough. Once I've got your attention I've got my meal ticket, because attention is energy in disguise. Your lovely energy, all that free power, comes over my way and I can hoover it up.

It may not be a disaster story that does it, of course. There's plenty of other ways of doing drama too. We can bully each other or take one another on guilt trips. We can batter each other with questions and demands, or look down from a great height on those who could quite well do with our affection or our advice. On the whole, when the drama is running, the odds are that anger – deeply hidden – is the fuel that keeps the show on the road.

Anger is a tricky energy. It's crude on the surface – the red face, the wrinkles – but underneath it's wily as a fox, hiding away so we don't catch sight of it. It props up the ego no end. But then, just suppose we dare to go inside, to dig beneath the rubble that clutters our internal space. What then? If we dig deep enough, we shall find a pinpoint of light, the still small voice of calm, like the eye at the centre of the hurricane. There's really only one way to get there, and that's through meditation. It's through the quiet rhythms and the natural wisdom of the body that the mind can eventually be stilled.

I can't pretend that I often embrace a meditative state in the frozen and sodden space that calls itself our home. No, that generally happens only in the Manor. We teach what we need to learn and even in spite of myself, I'm learning. Sometimes, from that inside place that's seeking light and calm, come little hints of something coming towards us from the outside: a change, a whiff of new oxygen, a glimmer of light.

"Dig deep, girl," says that quiet little voice from somewhere deep within. "It's not as bad as you think. Look at that light; it's only just at the end of the tunnel!"

"Nah. I'd say it's the headlamp of an oncoming train."

"But it's not," says the voice. "Promise. Just swap your lenses again and take a closer look."

And so I begin: I dare to go a little deeper still, right into the pain. I start to trust the pain, to embrace it, and it softens just a little.

I squint. I wriggle. I feel a breath of something like fresh air moving through my heart.

"You're headed for the land of the rising sun."

21

The Far East

That's what they call Japan: the land of the rising sun. Strung across a long chain of islands, it is one of the most beautiful landscapes on earth, with its misty, snow-capped peaks, its forests and tumbling mountain streams.

As for Tokyo, with all its steel and glass, it's an architect's futuristic paradise: skyscrapers in every shape and form; fountains, mirrors, twinkling lights in every nook and cranny. For a city girl in deep starvation, this is nothing short of a dream come true.

Two city girls, in fact: I'm here with Nicola. I insisted on that.

Believe you me, this commitment to come here was the hardest decision of my life. It happened like this:

I'm doing my thing, love, light and rainbows, all of that: teaching what I most direly need to learn. Bottles are exploding all over the place – that's what happens when the energies start whooshing and you've got the whole group focused on, say, Romola's key choice, the bottle in the middle with the magenta and that beautiful yellow-gold. That stuff that's been building up inside her starts welling to the surface and she's *feeling* it. You're chatting on, all about her repressed wisdom and her overly-developed tendency to do it all for the rest of them; or her terror, perhaps, of speaking up – and the feeling she's had that there's never anyone around to calm her down; or how she can reclaim all the humour and the joy in her life if she remembers there's all the support she needs out there, just the moment she decides to let it in. Or the conflict between her feisty fun-loving nature and the conditioning that says she must work 24.7. That kind of thing.

Bang!

That little bottle with magenta and gold has been feeling it too, all this stuff that's coming up from somewhere inside Romola, because everything is conscious – the trees and the flowers and even the *stones*. So all those words with all their energy have been piling up inside the brave little body of this bottle, with the light-messages it holds, and now it can't hack it any more. It's burst out of itself like a stressed-out volcano.

So now there's mess everywhere. These oils and herbal waters are so attractive when they're nicely contained in their bottles: broken glass and slippery stuff is another thing entirely. Better this, though, than have Romola explode – all she's doing is wailing like the cat just died.

There's one young woman who's watching it all as she sits recording it methodically – tape after tape – on a little portable machine, and she's silent as a mouse. It's because she's come all the way from Japan and she doesn't understand a word I've said. She probably thinks there's a mechanical device inside the bottle and it went wrong. But they work hard, the people of this valiant nation. While the rest of the group spends the evening swapping stories about their soul-mates or their would-be soul-mates ("his *eyes*; they're so deep and far-away – it's definitely the first time he's been on this planet"), and their spirit guides, Takane is up in her bedroom, slaving away as she transcribes the day's talk-show in a language of which she barely speaks a word.

She has come over here because her business partner has seen an article in a glossy women's magazine – those pretty bottles glinting like jewels all over the page – and he has spotted an opportunity.

We're still in the mid-nineties at this point and this Far Eastern country has a nickname: the land of the rising yen. So they send Takane over to England for total immersion, and at the end of her strange week in an ancient Manor House she approaches me and says,

"I invite you come working in Japan. You teach many peoples."

Well blow me down. I run it by the wizard and he comes up with a plan. The Japanese don't do things by halves, we all know that. So this is clearly the start of something. And there we are, with our frozen washing up liquid, our moise poison, our dripping walls...

"Take up teaching over there and you'll climb out of the poverty trap," says Gabriel. "If you put the children into boarding school, you can take the system out there and get it going. There are other new countries, too, waiting in the wings. The company will keep you on a basic salary and we'll always make sure there's enough work. We'll get you on the high-paid end of things: groups of 250 from time to time of an evening, on your way home, for half a year's rent. It's way the surest route to getting a home of your own again."

My brothers went to boarding school; it's not something I'd do to my worst enemy's worst child. Ah but those places have changed, I'm told. They're all warm and caring now. They've even got heating.

It's some suggestion, this: not the kind of thing we're in a position to turn away lightly either. It's family conference time.

"I don't want to do it," says Stephen, "but it's probably a good idea. I might as well admit I shan't pass a single exam this way."

He's reversed his decision to pass on the grass lately. It tends to be his major occupation these days, that and his guitar. His brain cells are checking out faster than rabbits check in.

Magdalen's not nine yet. And she's still wearing her hat.

"I'll do it, Mum!" she says. "I'll help you build."

Like I said, it was the most grizzly decision of my life.

So here we are in Tokyo, Nicola and I. We're in a posh hotel with seventeen restaurants to choose from. There's a piano inside our two-room suite, and a bathroom like the ones in the magazines, all clean and warm with a bath that shoots water and bubbles at you as you lie and go all zen. If you sit down to pee it's even better: push a little button and the seat warms up.

We like this place. We like it a lot, especially when we go out and find the cherry blossom in full bloom. Those flowers are famous for their frail, ethereal beauty; now we know why. We look at enchanted gardens and soak up the beauty of huts and temples, their gently curving wooden rooftops poised like ballerinas. Landscape design must have started in this magical place. Actually it did.

And the food! The critic Roland Barthes described a tray of Japanese food as a work of art in reverse – it arrives as a painting which, on being disturbed according to the rhythm of eating, becomes a palette. Painting and palette, both are sublime.

"The Japanese housewife aims to feed her family on thirty-seven different foodstuffs daily," our guide has explained.

Lentils and cabbage are out. Sushi and sashimi are in, with all the wakabe and all the ginger and all those thirty-seven other things. Yes please, we'll have the lot. This has got to be the best food in the world. No wonder they all live to a hundred and five.

Our host is a solemn, bespectacled young man. He reminds me of the gangly Catholic priest who was commissioned to instruct me in the faith when I was a giggling thirteen-year-old reluctant to listen to his earnest attempts to explain the true meaning of love. Our new friend's English is hesitant but passable, which is more than you can say for my Japanese. And he's keen to talk business as he passes the soy sauce.

"I am very exciting," he says.

Ah, so are we. Yes, we're exciting too.

22

Far from home

I have a confession to make. It has to do with the things I was thinking – those careless moments of "I wish," before that moment when the Japanese request arrived and we all jumped into cars and jet planes. Oh do be careful what you wish for.

Lone parenting is not so easy, you see, as most of you who have done it for any length of time will surely agree. The divine children I've been blessed with are my best, best friends; we're none of us in any doubt about that. I'd say that for the most part I'm their best friend too. That's not necessarily the same thing as being cut out for full-time solitary child-minding, 24-7 for years on end. Even the very closest of friends have more fun together if, just occasionally, they do something else.

So it was three years on from the day I set off in search of freedom and I was more than a little frayed at the edges – that's the polite version. I was in that chilly rectangle thing at the back of the house, the one with a tap and a space for a cooker, racking my brains on the question of food. More than that, I was racking my body on the question of inner fuel. At that moment I was so bone weary I didn't believe I could find the life force to cook another meal for the rest of time, not even if you gave me back my Laura Ashley kitchen-diner and my Italian tiles.

I was begging for respite, but convinced I had to earn it. There was no such thing as a free holiday in this life: my belief system was quite clear on that.

So in this reckless, unguarded moment I said, "Please, please give me a break. I'll do as many consultations as you like. Please can I not have to cook another meal – just for a *while*."

I said this in a deeply private place, of course – right in the solitude of my mind. I was far too tactful to say it out loud. But they heard it. No, not the children: the Team Upstairs. And they acted at once. Now some people say the unconscious has no sense of humour; it takes you literally. I'd say it has quite a substantial sense of humour, not to say downright mischief. And it's right out there in close touch with the mighty forces of the Universe.

"OK," says the Universe, like the genie that bursts out of Aladdin's oil-lamp. "That's what she asked for; that's what she gets."

So here I am in Tokyo, faster than you can say mouse dropping. I'm all alone in a bedroom the size of a dog kennel (the posh hotel? – that was the grand entrance; now it's time to get real).

"You make me heelah!" says Takane the businesswoman, a shade of irritation clouding the smile that greets me when I arrive for my second visit.

"Since two week they call me all the day – so much phone calls – they ask consultation. 'When Philippa come?' they say. They tell me plob-rem. I not like plob-rem!"

"OK," I reply. "I do problem, you do the rest. It's a deal."

And so the "problems" spill out, dissolved by colour, swimming towards the surface and the light. Stories of abuse, repression, confusion and grief: human beings are the same all over the globe. Sometimes fine layers of designer clothing conceal their pain; but not for long. At the high end of a Japanese city or in the cracked poverty and decay of a post-communist suburb, the laser beams of colour shine their light on the core issues of a shared humanity.

I don't speak the language, the languages. I'm fully dependent on the interpreter for the words. But it's my body that's doing the work, processing "plob-rem" like a cosmic launderette. I wake at night in floods of tears, or a fit of anger perhaps: either way, I know full well when these emotions are not my own. So I return to sleep, but when I arrive at work, what do I find? Ninety percent of the group in deep grief or exploding with rage. Okay, let's clear it then: a meditation; an exercise. Rome wasn't built in a day, but here the colour both excavates and reconstructs. We can make a start.

I'm nine thousand miles from everyone I love, in fact the ones I love the most are the ones I've dumped in boarding school. The hours are all upside down, which renders well-nigh impossible the task of dovetailing their hours with mine on the international phone lines. Besides, I'm in the land of the rising yen: try putting that call on your credit card if you've got one (I haven't).

Ah, but I eat at restaurants now. No cooking! Friday Italian, Saturday Thai, Sunday Chinese, Monday Japanese (very delicious, thank you), Tuesday Korean, Wednesday... you get the picture. The long-suffering interpreter comes along too, of course, every night, and she's done a twelve-hour shift just like I have. We've talked and talked and listened and listened through morning, afternoon and evening – first the day's teaching, then the private consulting sessions, one person at a time – and now we must talk and listen some more. So who's going to keel over first?

I'm swimming, floating, in a sea of nausea and fatigue; I can scarcely prop my eyelids open: I fear it will most likely be me.

"Excuse me, hello-o? Anybody out there – hello-o-o-o? Um, perhaps I was a bit hasty on the no-cooking bit..."

It's some logistical operation, this. If you entrust the most precious thing you have to the care of someone else then you have at least to ensure that the someone else can be trusted. You have to believe that they'll care. So you search the country for the one that will tick your boxes. Ah, but will you tick *theirs*? I have a boy here who will pass on the history, thanks, oh and the geography and the maths. A little cooking and sewing will do nicely. This is not the kind of thing that will impress the headmaster of an English public school. Anyway, I've found the schools in the end, so there are my children, arranged in a perfect triangle, each separated from the next by 150-odd miles; and every third weekend is an open one, otherwise known as an exeat: good, that means they can come home – have to, in fact.

So I'm a regular commuter – or an irregular one. I drive around the English towns and countryside, depositing these three budding geniuses in their scattered institutions, and then I drive to the airport: a round trip of three or four hundred miles a time. I line up with my baggage in the airport queue, waiting for my long-haul flight and reach the Far East 24-odd hours later, where I collapse in a shattered, jet-lagged heap. Then I do my 14-hours-a-day routine, sopping up the group's traumas and desolations for 19 days, perhaps (sometimes 15, sometimes more). Nauseous and faint with exhaustion, I jump on the next long-haul for the school round. My head afloat in an ocean of jetlag and weariness, I drive another three hundred miles, and we arrive back in the village with all the logs and firelighters we can pack into the car's spare spaces, stop at the front door to unpack the sticks and dash inside to light a fire in record time before we all die of exposure or damp rot.

"Had a nice holiday?" calls a friendly neighbour as we unpack the car.

Then we all pile under the covers and go to sleep. We spend a tearful, joyful, and as fun-filled weekend together as we can possibly whisk up before the whole thing starts again.

Once in a very long while, some generous person invites my children for one of those 'exeat' weekends when they have to leave their boarding establishments, which means I hang in there, over in the Far East, for four or five whole weeks.

And this is the real test. It's the big one, the one where you miss your loved ones like you're locked inside an igloo and you get to live with your self: you've got no place to run.

I'm here, a million miles from everyone and everything that I care for: for all I know, I might as well be on another planet. The grief is existential, personal, circumstantial – you name it I've got it. This is a beautiful country and a fascinating culture and it's one hundred per cent *other* in every way that I can possibly define.

The people here see me, quite rightly, as their teacher: they're paying me to be here and I have a job to do. They are attentive and thoughtful and polite and kind. It's not their job to stand in as a wizard or a mother too.

I get your problem, Dorothy, I really do. I've hit *Oz* and I want to go ho-o-o-ome. Problem is I'm none too sure where that is; in fact I no longer have the faintest idea. Here I am, surrounded by people from dawn to dusk – exhausted by people – and the solitude is like ice.

I'll get back to my family in a few weeks' time with just enough 50-pound notes in my back pocket to pay those school fees, and the rent, late in both cases but the bursars and accountants will put up with that. Climbing out of this frozen hole is going to be tough.

So here I am in my hotel box-room and I ought to be relieved and grateful for the peace and aloneness after my 14-hour day and I'm not. My mind is a whirlwind of chaos, darkness, angst. How am I going to get my family back home to where they belong? How am I going to make it up to them for everything they've lost? And how am I going to do this solitary confinement on Planet East: 31 days to go and I'm checking my watch every half hour.

I'm learning a simple truth: that anger, depression, terror, loss, despair, almost any brand of emotional pain; they are not about our environment, or the other people, or the way our lives look on the outside. They are about us, every time: wherever we go our selves have an annoying little way of coming along for the trip. Heave yourself off to another planet and the Wicked Witch will ride right along beside you.

"Hee hee. Cackle cackle. You just try getting away from *me*!"

It's that darkness thing again; it's confronting the shadow. Bertrand Russell said something about a choice: we can think or we can die, and most people choose death, in one form or another. Right now, I don't have that option. And for me, right here in this moment, there's nowhere to hide, either. This situation offers none of the buffers of a regular life to distract you from yourself. It's you and your thoughts, period.

It's efficient, this total-immersion method of encountering yourself – I will say that. Some people have kind of grumbling, ongoing nervous breakdowns, or lingering depressions, which cripple them for years. A few months of this, though, this solitary spiritual confinement, would kill me. I could never sustain the pain for that long. This is a do or die, and I've already taken a decision on that.

So here it is, my anger, my resentment, my terror, my deep rejection of myself. Here are my petty jealousies, my guilt, my griefs, my regrets, my desolation. They're wriggling through my veins and drilling at my nerve-ends. All of this is just one piece, maybe, in this work of excavating old foundations, digging up the old and outworn patterns of belief and errors of thought: there'll be more to come, of course. It's a substantial piece, nevertheless.

I'm remembering what my friend Michael told me all those years ago in Oxford: "Trouble with you," he said, "is you'd rather be in heaven than on earth. Get your feet on the ground. Bend your knees as you do the washing up!"

Ah, so that's the thing, is it? Getting down to ground level; even enjoying being at ground level, wherever you are. Sometimes I'm in the snow-bound sticks of England, sometimes I'm in the high-rise Tokyo blocks. Sometimes, these days, I'm in Prague, for that matter, or Dusseldorf or Budapest: the location makes no difference in the end – but maybe the truth is that, wherever I am, I hover. Maybe floaty people float because they fear that landing would be just a little too painful.

Here's a chance to land, a big one, though – a chance to learn from the tortoise and be at home with myself. If I can do that here, so far outside my comfort zone, then I can surely do it anywhere.

Home is where the heart is, after all – it's that place of truth that's often so hard to find, right inside ourselves. We can find it if we silence the shrill demands of the ego and surrender to a higher power. The ego will try every trick in the book to tell us we're alone; but the heart knows better: it knows there *are* no real separations, anywhere.

I'm feeling the pain anyway, the darkness, the fear: there's no choice attached to any of that. But I can choose my response to it. I can choose to fight it, resist it, suppress it; or I can embrace it. I can soften into it a little and make it my friend. I can breathe, for instance; I can consciously breathe. There's hours to go, after all, before light will break through the blinds and call me up for the next day's round. I can take the breath, the present moment, deep into my body; deep into the life of my cells.

This breathing, reaching into the depths of my lungs, my fingers, my heart, my toes, is only what my old friend Michael told me to do years ago; but I was far too busy. It's only what Gabriel told me to do; but my mind was on loudspeaker. It's only what Edwin told me to do; but it made me cry. Well here, I'm crying already, so what's the difference? I may as well stay with it and see what happens.

This gentle meditation, this focus on the rhythmical movement of the breath, has its own music: it is freeing me from mental chatter and carrying my attention deep into my body instead; it's calming me down. I read somewhere that the body has greater wisdom than the mind: maybe it's really so; maybe the body knows something that the monkey-mind is far too busy to notice.

This still place, located right in the heart of the body, is truly where the present moment lives. What does it matter *where* we are? Nothing changes until we change. Is this body-sense the thing they mean by "grounding"? Perhaps heaven's real location is right here on earth – in the here and the now. Come to think of it, where else could it possibly be?

It's a gift, this strange land with its ethereal landscapes and rising towers. It has its own way of reaching to heaven. I come over to this beautiful country time and again and always there is something new. So now, I'm discovering havens of tranquillity I've never imagined. These are not the places where tourists go, like the ones I've seen in Thailand.

Dotted around the backstreets, here and there, is a lotus in the city: a temple where real monks live and pray. I have a new friend, too, the great Buddha of Kamakura. Now *there's* some staying power in a storm. He used to be enclosed inside a temple, but that was 700 years ago, before a tidal wave washed away every last stone around him. Trust me, I know the feeling. But he stood firm, in all his bronze magnificence and glory. You can even go and spend some time inside him; you can climb his inner stairs.

I'm sitting *outside* him now, right beside him in the sun and there's a mini-earthquake shifting the ground beneath me. But I'm happy, as I rest comfortably in his shadow. I'm not meditating here in any formal way but I'm quiet and I'm still. There's a storm brewing out there, but just for the time being I could sit in this spot for years and years. I like it; it feels safe, it feels good.

I may be struggling: all those bills to cover in the space of the time I've grabbed between the precious weeks and months of school breaks, holidays, half-terms. Yet I'm building up something more powerful; I'm growing some capital of my own.

I may not know it yet, but this thing I'm doing, facing the darkness and making friends with my demons – though I say it myself, it's probably the most radical work we ever do.

23

One step at a time

Things are not going so well for Magdalen. We're into the part that no-one has warned us about. She was sent home, miracle of miracles, a few years ago: finished, over, done. Next?

We got the message, then: we were on our own. She's had headaches, of course, from the start. That's standard in brain injury: daily, relentless and mounting. I found that out from books. The learning difficulties are equally obvious. Addition and subtraction are double dutch to her now, and computers just landed off Mars; they came in with the aliens. They scramble her brain like nothing else.

And that limp: this was there from the start as well. It started as a foot that dragged, and on a snippet of a six-year-old body it's something you try to take as lightly as she does. She even ran quite fluidly for a few months, before the scar tissue began its deadly growth. But now it's getting worse.

I've known from the moment we got home to the cottage that coming back from the dead was only the beginning; the real test would be staying here, hanging in on the journey ahead. I didn't know the mechanics, the subtle workings of scar tissue on the brain and the nervous system, but I saw on a daily basis that to remain in her body this child was drawing on the deepest reserves of her soul.

She's done a few years in school.

"Quick," she hears the kids whisper to one another. "If we run fast she won't be able to keep up."

They're gone; she's alone. It's the life she's growing accustomed to. As she moves into her teens, there will be far worse persecution to face than this.

But now there are these endless abdominal pains. I'm

summoned to the hospital so I fly home. She has been admitted as a query appendix emergency – *that* again. It's not, though. By the time I arrive, the doctors assure me they've checked for everything they can think of and no, at least there's no infection: sorry, they've no idea what's wrong. I arrive at the bedside to find a nurse pouring antibiotics down Magdalen's throat and I grab it from her hand.

"She has no infection," I tell her.

"Yes I know; we're just making sure…"

"No."

I'm not the most popular person on the ward but I'm thanking my lucky stars that this was just the first dose and only the first few drops went down. She's been messed with quite enough by *life*, this child: no-one's going to mess with her immune system too. They are doing their best, these people; it's all they know.

I need to check out the scene, so we visit a consultant neurologist. He's a very gentle man, who clearly has children of his own. He examines Magdalen sympathetically and lovingly, and prepares a report: it doesn't make for good bedtime reading. She will grow steadily worse with each passing year, it reads; she will never walk easily and she'll certainly never run. We can anticipate a wheel-chair as mobility becomes more limited. As for the learning difficulties, they certainly won't improve. And the abdominal pain? He can't explain that. Perhaps we'd best book in with gastro-enterology.

We'll pass on gastro-enterology, thanks. I've had enough bad news for one day. I don't tell the surgeon this; he's far too kind and good.

But Magdalen is up with the lark. She's no idea what the medical report has said but she's overturning it anyway. She's out there, every day, on the school playing fields. Slowly, laboriously, she's running, one step at a time, right around the pitch. Not just once, mind. She's preparing for the school sports day and she's not about to be left out. And the teachers make sure she gets a place; she gets a head-start of a few hundred yards and ends up not too far behind.

Besides, we can change the past, can't we? I know that. I'm not running this proposition by the neurological surgeon, I admit – kind though he is. I'm not planning on getting myself certified; I'm needed too much at home. I'm just keeping this crucial information right at the front of my own mind and shielding my child from suggestions that won't help the situation any. Let's just watch those seeds we're planting, right?

So I find a little angel, a quiet French girl called Ghislaine. She's a cranial osteopath and she's training to be a doctor, too. She loves children and she makes Magdalen laugh. They're movie buffs, both, and they swap views on what's happening over in Beverley Hills.

"And don't worry about those rotten girls at school," Ghislaine tells her. "No-one likes to see someone who's dealing with their limitations. It reminds them of their own limitations, the ones they're not dealing with – far too uncomfortable."

She's got good news for us. Oh yes, there's a perfectly good explanation for all those aches and pains. Brain can't connect with foot; it's way too seized up with scar tissue, right up in the place where all the messages start. So foot doesn't get to move properly and how can the lymph drain then? Now the pressure builds up in the liver and kidneys fit to scream. Oh and the spasm – that lower leg is held rigid like wrought iron and the ankle will hardly move; but that doesn't stop the foot from cramping 24 hours a day. It's hard to sleep when your toes curl up the whole time and send those shooting pains up your leg. That's the scar tissue too: the brain's all irritated from the pressure on it so the nerves go hyper.

"We're getting it moving, though," she adds, as she talks now to me. "It will take some years, but hang in there. Get her through to her twenties and you'll be amazed."

And now I'm remembering my silent agreement with my child, my agreement with myself:

"You can change the past. It will be as though the accident never happened."

"Nonsense," says the world. "The earth is flat: after all – we just *know* it."

And check this: "the telephone has too many shortcomings to be seriously considered."

As for "heavier than air flying machines," they're impossible: the President of the Royal Society told us so himself, way back in 1895.

"Everything that can be invented has been invented," the commissioner of the US patent office told us that a long time ago, too – in 1899.

In a few years from now, I shall discover what some more of those clever people have been doing and saying – the scientists who are pushing the frontiers further with every passing day. I shall learn that they have been collecting data, electronic or biological, and storing it for a few days or months before getting people to use their minds to influence the data. At which they point those data change. I shall Google "Retroactive Intentional Influence" and find 294,000 entries. What does the phrase mean? It means that prayer works, even when it's directed backwards in time.

> *Backward, turn backward, O Time, in your flight,*
> *Make me a child again, just for tonight.*

Elizabeth Akers Allen wrote that, in the late 19th century. It's a romantic notion, the gentle stuff of a whole generation of poets. Is this wishful thinking? Is it just the stuff of poetry? Or could even these simple words suggest a possibility about altering the way that we think? Can prayer, in fact, work retrospectively? And will we ourselves learn to bring our healing intentions to interact mentally with biological systems in a "backward" or time-displaced manner, in such a way that the outcome of what was set in place earlier is altered?

I don't know yet; I haven't even formulated the question. But one day in the future, the question will answer itself.

24

All change

Magdalen's isn't the only body that's struggling.

But surely it isn't the moment to worry about that now, as I sit in the early spring sunshine in Prague, for is there a more beautiful city on the planet? I doubt it. I'm sipping hot chocolate as I sit here and gaze. I don't know too much about what else this potent Emperor Charles IV did, but if you build a bridge like this one then posterity at least is grateful. And it's no wonder that Mozart couldn't stay away from the place. Those Baroque buildings, the Gothic structures, the magic at the heart of this city, would have been in place well before he paid his first visit. They'd have been looking much as they are now, like cottages and palaces built for angels.

It slices through the heart of Europe, this long, thin country with its lakes and plains, and its mountains covered in pine. The romance of Dvorak floats around the hills. It was a powerful kingdom once but it's quieter these days; more low key. I like it better that way. You can almost hear the notes of Mozart's piano echoing through the walls; clarinets and flutes floating down the river. You can feel the sounds in the air that you breathe.

It's nice and private here at crack of dawn, nice and quiet; just me and Mozart, the rippling water, the gargoyles, the walls of this golden city. Even the birds are quiet. All is silence, except for the little concert inside my head, and the chats.

"You didn't have too hot a time on this planet, did you, young Wolfgang? Or did you like it anyway, in spite of all of it? You did the grinding poverty; you did the jealous rivals too. It's a tough life."

The scenery distracts me for a while but not for long. It's the *new* countries I've been assigned, as little by little the fruits of my labours in Japan have been handed over to others. These are places where nothing is established: you have to create a market as well as cater for it, and most of these colour-bare countries are recovering from a communist regime. The 'high-paid end of things' that was promised, those fertile stop-overs on the way home, somehow never showed up in the end.

"Yes," I've said to my teacher, "but to keep the school bursars happy we need twenty students on every course, not ten. And Eastern Europe is recovering from *total repression*. They can't even pay their *own* bills – why choose their economy to fix mine?"

I'm rushing around the planet at the speed of lightning and I'm scarcely making ends meet. What's more, you can batter a body just so far but each body has its limits, and mine is breaking down fast. Standing up is a problem: I can only do it for a few minutes at a time. Sleep? Not much of that: I'm strung out with nervous exhaustion. Food? That's a tricky area too: there's too much pain in my gut; can't hold much inside. Have I got cancer? No, just pre-cancerous cells all over the place. Dicey cells lurking, threatening: "Please arrange to see the Consultant for further tests." No thanks, I'll not resort to that just yet: I'll do it my way.

Just stay on top of the fainting attacks and keep on going: that's the spirit.

The angels thanked me most graciously the other day, through a floaty friend, for the work I'm doing and added that it's the hardest work there is. Well, thanks for that, but do I have a choice?

My Japanese hostess has grown alarmed at the state of my health, so she's taken me to a doctor. They're way ahead of us over there: all the physicians are using those Radionics machines. You hold a thing in your hand and it tracks every system in your body; every organ too. Then they give you a printout which tells you the news. Except that this one is written in Japanese, which I still don't speak or understand. I've not moved beyond page one of my phrase book.

There's a deathly silence as the doctor examines this piece of paper. His face falls through the floor and rapidly re-arranges itself. And then he has a chat with Takane. Her face falls too.

"He say he much worry," she tells me.

Here's the score: worst exam result I ever had. The organs and systems in my body are burnt out – the whole lot. There's no way, the doctor says, that I can be standing up – well on the whole I'm not. The work I'm doing? It's simply not possible: agreed. There's one thing the doctor doesn't understand at all: no cancer – it's a *miracle*, he tells her, a *miracle*. The doctor's getting excitable now, as he spills out to her all in a rush.

"This woman," she says, translating his words as he goes, "she so much is protecting from angel."

They're something else, these Japanese doctors. They are full-on medicine men but they're smart enough to embrace the most ancient of wisdom as well as the newer tricks. He mixes a remedy and says it may help a little.

I'm not surprised by any of it, just stuck for solutions.

We've all escaped the jaws of death already, though, me and my three friends; we're artists at survival. I'm damned if I'll give in now. Something has to change, it's obviously not negotiable. And that's what I'm thinking here in the heart of Europe, a few weeks later, as I drink my hot chocolate along with those gentle, ghostly echoes of piano and violin. It's time for the next plane soon, and a few days with the kids.

So I get back to that damp place which, just for the moment, almost feels like home. I'm thinking I'll book in with the wizard and let him know the scene. He's a healer, after all, and full of magical powers. He'll probably have some inspiration to share, some magical solution. Oh and there's something else: a few months ago, he asked me to write a book – in my spare time, you know. He wants me to write a book to tell people all about the miracles of colour healing.

"Spare *time*?" I've gasped, inwardly.

But I've done it anyway. Obedient to the letter, I've sent him a copy of the final draft. The publishers love it, but will he? It's the wizard's word that matters, after all. Have I got it *right*?

So here I am with the wizard, otherwise known as Gabriel, the very man who worked so hard to save the life of my child, and the first thing I discover is I've lost my job. The company will no longer support me; I'll not be needed in Japan any longer; finito; curtains; this is *it*.

I'm out of my depth here. I don't understand the words I'm hearing. My ears are moving in and out of the dream-state, my eyes hovering between reality and fog. "Company tightening its belt." (*The fleet of Audis?*) "Basic maintenance not possible." (*The markets set up for decades to come?*) "Other teachers want Japan; Finish the projects you're on; Exchange rate awfully difficult these days." The words drift on: meaningless, devoid of truth.

What do I do? (*Oh, some consultations – you can always do those.*) What do we live on? (*Your problem – you'll think of something.*) Where do we live? Cardboard boxes at the railway station?

"Lift your fledglings out of ruin and desolation and build them a life." This is the package I was sold. So what, exactly, did I do wrong? I did what I was told: took the colours around the world; set up the markets; wrote a book.

I'm aware that the world I've been working so expensively to construct around us all these years has just collapsed into rubble around my feet. But shock makes you dumb as well as stupid. There's three small lives I must carry through this – three youngsters established in fee-paying schools, facing exams that will steer the course of their lives. But I'm heavy, earthbound, numb; divorced from my senses, I can't think, let alone speak.

Where do we go? Back to the mercy of HM Government: there's clearly no choice. And no escape from this hell-hole in the desert in the sticks: we've nothing left to sell.

Ah, but Dorothy thought the wizard was a wizard. He would sort it all out, wouldn't he? He would show her the way home; he would take her there, right back over the rainbow. She was wrong, of course. He was a man, like the rest of us; just a little man, behind a screen.

He left Oz, after all, without her, in his well-inflated balloon; she had to make the next lap of the journey on her own. She was learning a simple, fundamental truth: we all have to learn to map-read for ourselves. We have to float our own balloons.

I thought I knew anger before but that was grade one stuff; the starter package. Now I'm learning what anger really means. He's a brave man to play Judas because I shall not forgive him for years.

And years.

But one day – way in the future – I shall dig deep and find that forgiveness from somewhere; and when I do, it will be because I've understood: I will know in my heart, not my mind, that there are no victims. I will know that hatred is arsenic for the soul; it's a poison that shrinks and diminishes us.

I will understand that forgiveness is the single quality above all others that makes us fully human.

I will know in the cells of my body that all the world really is a stage and all the men and women merely players.

I will understand that it is we who set up the dramas every time; that we do it so that we shall find our Selves.

Furthermore, I will know that those who play Judas are the catalysts: they may be a violent father, a jealous teacher, a manipulative spouse; but perhaps we must each thank our own Judas – whatever part he or she may take in our own particular story – for playing a sacrificial role, for loving us enough to be hated in life, for without them it's quite likely that we would never search deep enough inside to find our own drums and beat them, to play our own tune.

Perhaps, too, there was another reason for those years of migration. I've watched as broken lives around the globe gently rebuild themselves under the warming rays of colour and of light. Maybe, in the process, I have gained a little knowledge too;

maybe some of those healing rays have found their way through to me.

Maybe, somewhere in the darkness of my heart and soul, a seed is germinating, growing: one day, maybe, it will sprout; pour out the fruits of the Universe. For the real nature of the Universe is love; it is joy, and abundance and knowledge and truth.

It's a set-up, a story, all of it: we set it up to entertain ourselves and then we get lost in the drama of it all. We forget who we were, who we really are. But what better tool for learning than a good story? And finding they've left without you. There's no balloon here after all; but don't worry, Dorothy, says the Good Witch: just click your heels together three times. The power of the Holy Trinity is right there within you. Brahma, Vishnu and Shiva: they're all there inside. You can find your own way home. It's called growing up.

Don't try telling me any of this at this moment, though, not yet. Bankrupted on every possible level, swaying in an earthquake of shock and betrayal, scarcely knowing where to find the next breath, I'm seized up with anger and hatred, terror and sheer disgust: I won't believe a word you say.

For here I am back in Tokyo now and autumn's arrived: the perfect season for finishing the projects I'm on. I'm sitting down, of course; I won't be standing for a while yet. And I have fourteen dedicated students scribbling down every word I say: I'm God, you see, because I'm the teacher. That's the way it works in this culture: it's not personal; it goes with the job – and they don't even *know* that God's out of a job. They don't know that the lives of God's children have been shattered and crushed; that God's body is caving in further by the day. The phone rings and it's an emergency call from Magdalen's school. She's been working so hard to get that body of hers doing all the stuff; there's nothing she won't do to join in again. So in her Trojan attempts to do life like everyone else, she's fallen off a wooden horse in the gym and broken her arm.

I can picture the whole scene, sense each detail of it in every nerve of my body: I can feel every ounce of effort and emotion that this child, once the fastest runner on the block, has put into a task that's well-nigh impossible. The hard bleak isolation, the cold unfeeling light that shines upon her life in school: the taunting of the children; the frosty impatience of plenty more of her teachers than one. It's coursing through my body like shards of broken glass. Her teacher puts my child on the line to speak to me and she's wailing.

The trouble is, so am I.

In this culture that doesn't happen. I'm out in the corridor, naturally, as far away from those students as I can get; and I'm swallowing the sounds I'm making, of course, as deep as I can. And the earnest young businessman, mein host – the exciting one – is standing there looking like I've lost my mind and he tells me, "But it eess broken arm only. I breaking my arm when I am young. It mend later."

Yes of course: broken arm, mend later. How simple. And you know what I'm about? Communication: that's my thing; it's how I earn our *living*, for goodness' sake. And there's no way in a million years of Sundays that I will ever explain to this kind and well-intentioned fellow that there is a valid reason why their usually-rational God has dissolved in a blubbing heap. It's obvious to him that their teacher's marbles have just run right out.

I've had enough of this fiasco. I'm giving in and giving *up*. There must be some kind of answer up there.

25

Coming home

The plane will leave Tokyo tomorrow and I've not spotted an altar anywhere in these parts under which I could possibly hide, even if I had the time to do so. But I have some paper and a pen. So I adopt a new strategy and I highly recommend it. The strategy is you write a letter to God.

It's different from just chatting, this, or pleading from your place of – well, whatever the place is in your particular case: desperation, helplessness, hopefulness, simple desire? What this letter does is it organizes your intentions and your thoughts. You can tell God very clearly what it is that you need. In doing this, you acutely focus your own intention. The Universe loves nothing better than clarity.

And there's something else: this has to do with how prayer works, particularly the kind where what we're aiming at is manifestation of some kind, fetching what seems like a preposterously unlikely possibility out of the ethers and having it show up for real.

First we have a thought, then we have a feeling engendered by that thought; now the feeling is what energizes the thought, so it's quite important to pay attention to this quality of feeling as well as the thought. Believe you me, what I'm feeling right here, right now, is nothing too tame and quiet: plenty of energy *there*.

The next step is you maybe speak your thought out loud – not under the altar, probably, but to a friend or someone else who loves you.

But then you can do this other thing. You write it down, and that's like laying the first brick of whatever it is that you're building – or intending to build.

The writing turns your thought, your feeling, your intention, into a *thing*. It's a thing already, of course, that thought – though we tend to forget this for most of the time. But this letter, this string of words, is a thing that you can touch and see. It gives substance and weight to the thoughts and feelings you want to express, and this means your message will go out with some considerable force.

So I write, and I write. I tell God about it – all of it: all of the feelings, all of the terror, all of the love and *all* of the need to survive; and I ask Him/Her or whatever this Force is to absorb all these feelings and purify them. It's pouring out like water from a garden hose; this He/She/It that I'm writing to, and as I do so, this Someone or Something doesn't feel so far away. It feels like my thoughts are heard, my words are seen. I'm feeling this Godness around me and inside me: it's *for* us, surely, this Mind behind the universe? It's through us and with us and in us, but it's for us too. It wants for us whatever it is that we truly wish for ourselves; it wants all that will serve the highest good of us and all the others around us. It really doesn't wish for us to feel abandoned, scared, alone.

"Come home," it says. "It's all right; never fear. Never Forget Everything's All Right."

I'm putting in my shopping list now. This is the bit about clarity: be careful what you wish for.

"Dear God," I'm writing. "I cannot do this any more. I cannot work at this body-wrecking pace. I cannot do this to my children. I'm *for* them – you know that and so do they – but I must be *with* them too. Please find us a way. Please give me a break. Please put us all together again. And just for the moment, we can't do this living-in-the-sticks thing any more. So here's another detail: please find us a place and a way of paying for this place, and for living, in a *city*. Please keep me alive, and please let us be alive *together*. Thank you, God. I love you, I really do."

So I pack up my letter, and then I pack my luggage too. This is the last time I shall be in the Far East for many years to come, I'm

137

fairly sure of that. I can't even think about this, though; I'm obsessed with the only thought that matters: "I'm going home."

There's more space in the aircraft than there will be in a few years' time, when the whole world will be flying like there's no tomorrow. I have a whole row of seats to myself. I can lie down if I choose. I can relax. I'm confident, convinced that I've been heard.

So I'm in this new space, not looking for a wizard any more: I'm talking to something far greater than that. There's a budding friendship here and it's growing as I speak. I feel held, I'm basking in the start of a great new partnership: me and God. He's right there in my heart and my heart is right there in his.

But here's the thing about close relationship. It creates a safe space for your wounds to come up and stare you – and soon enough your loved one, when that's a person – right in the face. Well we've got quite a thing going here, me and God. I'm feeling all safe and loved, but I haven't reckoned yet on the pieces that are hiding underneath, as the tight walls holding them there begin to soften and dissolve. Oh but now they're coming up, like a raging wave. You're going to have to hold me through this one, Whoever is out there – or in there. I'm forgetting *already*; Forgetting Everything's All Right. It's not all right at all.

I can't die *now*!!! What will happen to the children? They have no other parent, no grandparent. They may not have much of a roof but at least I put bread on the table (well, the floor – we sold the table). And all that is about to stop and they'll be out in the freezing cold with nothing to eat and nowhere to live because I'm going to *die* – anyone could tell you that, because the plane's about to crash! How can a plane possibly stay in the air, carrying all those people and all their luggage, for fifteen, sixteen whole hours? It's the silliest thing I ever heard. It's world-class, the blubbing, and it carries on all the way, thousand on thousand of air miles, over all the oceans and all the land.

"Ladies and gentlemen, please place your seats in the upright position for landing."

What? Oh my giddy aunt, I can see English rooftops out there: they're moving closer and closer. We're gliding downwards like a great swan, smooth as you please. We're actually touching down. Judder judder. You mean, we've *landed* and I'm not even *dead?* And the plane is still in one piece: not a wing broken, an engine exploded, a wheel rolling around? And even the sun has come out.

England, dear England. I love it: funny I've not noticed that so much before. Where's the car? Oh, I remember: I left it in that huge car park with the nice man I chatted to on the way out, weeks ago; the one with the chocolate-smooth skin and the bobble hat. I even left my keys with him. I'd better find that office.

"Hello!" someone calls. I turn around. It's him: the same man again. Bobble hat and all. "Yours was the old blue Passat, wasn't it?"

I nod, incredulous. There must be several thousand cars in this vast space.

"We had a few problems with the vandals," he goes on. "I put it over in that corner for you; I wanted to keep it safe."

They come in all shapes and sizes, the angels.

I'm driving now: that wonderful journey where I pick up the super-heroes waiting for me in school. The leaves are ochre and gold; autumn assails my senses from every side. And me? I'm calm as that hang glider over there, floating over the fields in the glinting sun.

And now we're back, in that old place with its worn-out thatch and yes it's freezing cold and wringing wet. But we rush around with our firelighters and our sticks. We pile on our five layers of woollies and welcome it anyway, every piece of it: the old fireplaces, the beams so low you'll crack your head, the tap that works. We snuggle into our beds and sleep is sweeter than those wonderful cherries my kind Japanese hosts gave me to bring home.

I awaken early, refreshed. Magdalen's the only one up. The

phone soon rings. We've been gone a few weeks; I didn't know they knew we're home. It's a lawyer from London. I knew him years ago, in those halcyon days when I could take a stroll through Hyde Park on a sunny afternoon. He's got news for me: he tells me this piece of news and I collapse in floods of tears.

Magdalen is playing in her special dolls-house corner and she's looking alarmed. Now you may think that I blub all the time but you're wrong. This child is used to a smiling face, and she sees me quite often: she should know. I can pull out my well-practised grin and polish it at the drop of a hat. But this new stuff, the wailing and sobbing: she's obviously finding it alarming.

"Mum – what's the matter?"

"We've been given some money!" I tell her. "We can go home!"

She comes over and puts an arm around me and her face looks thoroughly confused.

"Why are you crying then?"

That's not a question I can answer too easily. I scoop her up in all the arms and legs I can find and tell her that tears mean all kinds of things, that sometimes they mean happiness and relief like nothing – or one piece next to nothing – that you've ever imagined in all your life.

Comment

Marriage and the Soul

Some time early in the twenty-first century, I shall learn a piece of information that has the potential to change the lives of all of us, if we'll listen. It is this:

If you move your foot, say, or lift a pen from your desk, the neural impulse to act – the order to fire, if you like – is sent out before you have the thought to take the action.

Who, then, is taking the decision?

The mind is the place where ego lives; and the decision to act, it seems, is not taken by the mind.

If this is the case when we decide on something comparatively insignificant - lifting a fork or stirring the tea – this must certainly be a mechanism that is in place for the larger events of our lives. And if it's not the mind that's doing the talking, giving the orders, then what else is there?

Something greater is clearly in charge: this must be that thing which through the ages they have called the soul. The soul, surely, is running things; it's captain of the ship. The ego in all its glory – or all its despair – is merely following along the path that was set by a higher power before this little fellow in all its illusory separateness ever showed up at all.

Science has shown us that if we wish to understand the universe or ourselves, we really have to follow the evidence into the nebulous world of spirit. Other paths of research are arid; they yield nothing but confusion and a blank wall. So what do we mean by spirit? We mean the no-thing that comes before the some-thing. We mean the non-matter that comes before the matter. Spirit is that place where everything is merely energy and information, quantum soup. Or not merely, perhaps: maybe the power here is awesome; maybe here is the home of the animating force that's behind the entire created world.

So let's apply this knowledge to our life journeys, our stories. Let's look at the evidence – that the soul handles the things that happen, large and small – and remember that this nebulous, all-spirit aspect of us is the greater part of who we are. It's the aspect of us that stays in touch with the great ocean of spirit, that force which creates everything in the universe. It cannot *not* stay in touch with this force-field because it's a part of that field, inseparable. It never left home in the first place. Neither did we, of course – we just thought we did.

This has got to be good news. It suggests that behind the excruciating pieces, the problems, the pain, the hurdles in the lives of every one of us, there is in fact a plan. We can start to see the soul as a benevolent parent allowing the ego to run around like a rebellious teenager. The youngster believes that it's free-running the show, but the parent never abandoned its watch. The teenager's like a learner driver in a dual control car, where the soul, aka the instructor, has full command of the controls. The instructor has seen what's coming round the corner ahead of time: he's swift to respond and to plan. The teenager is in experienced hands.

This invisible instructor sits beside us – or behind us, before us, within us, perhaps – anticipating our every move. He, or she, shows us when to push forward, when to pull back. The learner takes a turn to the left; maybe she favours the comforts of the tree-lined avenue above the sharp lines of the high-rise blocks, and she believes that she's done it all alone. In an important sense she has done, because this is how it feels. Our subjective reality is crucial in any learning process.

Yet the learner, the individual self, is never alone. Our higher power already chose that left turn because it knew what lurked beneath its tree-lined façade. It saw the twists and turns that lay around the corner, out of ego-vision. It knew who and what lived and worked and played there, before our conscious mind had a chance to find out. We thought we flashed the indicator all of our own accord, but that invisible something out of nowhere sent the signal out already. The soul, of course, can modify its chosen route at any given moment; it is infinitely flexible in its response to the given conditions – and the ego will always follow, just behind.

So the ego is quite safe, as it takes us off down the road on one crazy adventure after another: a boring job, or one that drives us round the bend and up the wall; a battering love affair; a fight with addiction; a plummeting business. The ego is just getting out there so that the developing individual of which it is such an intricate part can get on with his or her lessons: meet the people, do the things she signed up for long ago, in some other dimension, some other framework of time and space.

The learning happens through the journey. Even the great teachers – Christ, Buddha, the prophets – didn't know what they were capable of before the events of their lives unfolded around them. To discover their courage, their compassion, generosity, commitment or loyalty, they had to navigate their way through their own life paths. They had to find out who they were; to do this, they engaged with all the hurdles, the satisfactions, all the joys and pains of physical existence.

As something similar to this begins to happen for you or for me, the ego begins to see the truth: that it's never been alone. Yes, it's had freedom of a kind: the right to make its own mistakes. This is what we mean, more or less, when we talk of free will. But in another sense its fortunes have been predestined all the way along – not by some impersonal force of fate but by the choices of the conscious soul from which that ego has sprung.

When you reach for the phone, then, or brake the car, your soul has waved the conductor's baton, before you stretch your hand or press your foot.

This is great news for an ego which – in spite of its best efforts to persuade us otherwise – is really very small and very scared. It can relax in the knowledge that its loving parent really does have it handled. We can make all the dumb decisions we like but the soul knows us far better than we know ourselves. It will be one step ahead of us all the way. And this means that – at the moment we are ready – this great loving parent is sure to bring us home.

True marriage is an inner process, not an outer one. As our fears and anxieties begin to dissolve, we soften and expand. Our consciousness awakens from a long sleep, and the idea that we were separate and alone evaporates into the nothingness from which it came. We cease to be afraid of the light that is our real selves; instead, we embrace it and we re-unite with it.

Sitting beside that phone in the old house with half a worn-out thatch on its sagging roof, as I laugh and cry in the wake of stunning and miraculous news, I know very little of the soul's awesome, gentle power.

And now a few weeks later, back in this strange, ancient, damp and really quite friendly house for the very last time, we're packing the boxes and bidding farewell to the frozen north. We're taking leave of our landlady: she shakes us by the hand and wishes us well.

"Oh and, er…" she adds with a hint of embarrassment, as we pile into the car and set off behind the removals van, "we've decided to install central heating."

"Good decision!" I reply.

If I had known the subtle truth of our neuro-spiritual physiology back then, if I had understood that in every move we are following the call of a power within us that's greater than anything our minds have dreamed of, I might have found this next lap of the journey that lay ahead of us a deal easier. I would have known that before the angels could fully enter my world and make their presence felt, bringing gifts greater than any wizard could ever do, I should have to dig a little deeper. An outer marriage was on the horizon but only as the inner one grew firmer.

It was not yet time for the retrospective lenses to lend their 20:20 insights.

I don't think that in these latter years of the closing century, even the scientists had yet discovered this crucial fact: that when we flick the light switch or reach for a spoon, the signal went out to fire before we had the thought. I knew only what I needed to know at the time: that at long last, we were homeward bound. At that moment, this was the only thing that could possibly matter at all.

Four

For months the prince wandered through the
wastelands.
One day, while Rapunzel sang as she fetched water,
the prince heard her voice again. When they fell into
each other's arms, her tears immediately restored his
sight. The Prince led her to his kingdom, where they
lived happily ever after.

26

November 1997

Let us rewind here, just to the moment of that phone call, because this next chapter is the stuff of fairy tales, not real life. The news brought by that magical call concerned a legacy, appearing completely out of the blue, from old friends who had stood in for me as parents 30 years before.

As we spend the weekend in the waterlogged, thatchless abode before we pile back in for the school round almost for the last time, we're reeling with shock, joy and disbelief. The next thing we know, I'm negotiating the bends of our bizarre school round and leaving the children scattered for the last time before I roll on to Oxford faster than you can say deep freeze. I'm blitzing every letting agency this old town's ever seen. There are ten houses to visit in two days: they're hideous, depressing, depressed; damp, cold, minute. No, I will not bring those super-heroes back to dumps like these, so I return to the office where my search began, because we must be in by Christmas and that's not many weeks away. And I must board another plane this afternoon.

So now, after these 48 hours of frantic house-seeking, I find there is just one more house to look at. It has mysteriously appeared on the market in these last few hours, its rent magically reduced to the upper end of our price bracket, and it fits us and suits us down to the last brick, floorboard and curtain rail. It's in a beautiful Regency terrace faced with gentle, golden stone, a stone's throw away from the centre of town. It's warm outside and in. The theatre is a mere 500 paces off; the cinema is 600 paces away; the park – a little further. Help is in sight, Mr Starbucks, 300 yards down the road: I'll keep you in business single–handed.

My prayer was seen; it was read, heard – and acted upon. The whole event is nothing short of miraculous.

Other people might say, "Nonsense. The cash you're about to receive was set in motion seven years ago, when your friend wrote his Will. It's pure chance that it has taken effect now, just when you need it the most."

And I will never agree with them, not in a million years. It is very clear that chance has nothing to do with any of it. I know this for certain sure, because I've not been with this property agent for many minutes, strolling around this heavenly house, upstairs, downstairs, outside and in, before it occurs to me that my friends, the adopted parents I lived with in London for so many happy years, had talked from time to time about the start of their married life in Oxford, just as the Second World War was coming to an end. They had reminisced about life in their home in town, just around the corner from the hospital and the library where they respectively worked. And that home was in this street, of course it was! – I've just remembered.

But then comes the flash. It was not merely in this street that they lived; it was in this house, the one I'm standing in. I've never had the remotest idea of where on this road my friends once lived – until this moment. I know it now, in every bone of my body. I call the only person on the planet who will know for sure, and within just a few hours it's confirmed. She sends me a letter, found in an old drawer, addressed to our mutual friends at the exact place that we're about to rent in the late 1990s: the postmark is 1945.

The odds against anything so impossible are outrageous – the number of houses in an average-sized town, the number available for leasing at *any* given moment, the timing of this sudden avail-ability together with the rare gift of funds, *their* funds, *their* house – are of lottery proportions. Besides, nothing on *this* beautiful terrace comes on the market ever: not for letting or for sale. These old friends who have died – one of them seven years ago and the other just the other month – and come to our rescue, have surely led me, via one property agent after another, right to the front door of the place they once loved so much, and they have provided the wherewithal for rent and food for quite a while to come.

So here we are, a few weeks later, just in time for Christmas. There's time now for a respite, while we dig around and re-bed ourselves a little. Nicola has left for university, the two younger children are rooting themselves in local schools. My last teaching assignment is complete; and so, more or less, is my physical collapse, as the adrenaline flooding of years on end at last dries up and gives way to every symptom of burnout in the book. On a very good day, I can walk a hundred yards. The other days, I'm more likely to be found under the covers, half asleep.

There's a new request from Hungary – please oh please bring the colour and the light.

"Don't even think about it," says Michael, my old healer and friend, "or I won't be able to keep you out of hospital."

So I must stay put. And here I still am, as winter breaks into a magically early spring, resting and being nourished back into life. I'm walking with my children now, in the grounds of a beautiful park, under a sapphire sky. As we picnic under a tree and sunbathe in the startling warmth of this February sunshine, gazing at a clear sky of pure sapphire through the soft new foliage, I'm reflecting on the miracle that has brought us back home. The coincidences, though, are not done with us yet.

I have a confession to make, you see. Maybe I should never have made fun of those people talking of soul mates and twin flames, because back in the sticks, I'd met someone who felt uncomfortably close to being something of the kind himself. I'd learned all about these flaming mates: they walk into your life and they blow it right apart – as if that hadn't been comprehensively achieved already. You've only met this person half a dozen times, say, and you find they've stopped your heart right in its tracks.

Or maybe it's something else they're up to. Maybe what they're really doing is setting your heart *alight*. Waking it up from the dead.

A single soul, goes the theory, divides itself in half, the better to gather experience in its journeys across the universe, or across the earth. Once in a while, the two halves will incarnate at the same time and if they meet, they are drawn together as surely as the poles of two opposing magnets. Like Stendhal said of beauty, this concept offers the promise of happiness. It seems to suggest the existence of the one mate who gets you. The idea is as beguiling as it is improbable, on a planet populated by six to seven billion souls.

Yet there's no doubt that life sometimes leads us into the path of another person in a way that is far from ordinary. We bump into that person and our existence is forever changed.

"When you meet your soul partner, you tend to find that everyone who comes into your life from then on is there for a reason. They're old friends and you're meant to meet up again and get together to do the thing you've come here to do. It's quite a comfort, discovering people who get you. Meeting your spiritual partner is the fillip to the soul, the thing that reminds you who you really are. It kick starts you on your path – the real one."

That was my old friend William speaking – the one who reads the stars. I've worked quite hard to get away from this person, you see, for a few years now. Not that there's anything to get away *from*: he's an honourable man, this John, and when we met he had other things to do. We were worlds apart. It was the love affair that never happened and quite right too: he has children and he loves them. He came to me for help and advice because he was not a happy camper. But horror of horrors, sparks started to fly, sparks that were different from the ones we'd known or felt before. No, this cannot be. Hang in there, Mr Twin Soul, and do your thing: the world is in desperate need of fathers like you.

So it was cheerio, have a nice life – oh and see you in the next one. And all of that was so long ago I've nearly forgotten it. Or tried to.

But soon, as we're settling into the new home, there comes another of those mind-blowing phone calls, from the man himself; because his life, like ours, is up for renewal so he's finding himself following in our footsteps to the south. He's battered and bruised – but no more, perhaps, than many of us are by the time we choose to wake up. And just like me, he's managed to lose more or less everything he ever owned. ("Very good for you": Alison's verdict rattles around my brain.) Moreover, just like us, John seems to have been led to this town by invisible guides: a random offer of a number of contractual jobs has brought him here. Yet not before he has been asked to repair the outcome of a contract that was set up back in the northern sticks, at least a hundred miles west of where we all lived at the time.

Well not quite all of us: one person had moved away to just this place, a hundred miles and more from all the frozen houses, and he was the one who set up the contract, which then went disastrously wrong. This person, it turns out, was none other than Mr Outward Bound himself. But check this:

Mr Soul Mate gets a call, from someone in the south, with a sudden request: will he join their team? Will he take on the trouble-shooting jobs required to sort out the corporate contracts that have gone disastrously wrong? It will entail travelling far and wide.

Will he just? He's up and ready for change, and this is the stepping stone he's been seeking. His case is packed; he's ready to go. Where first? To a town far away, a place he's never been, but the source of power stations and engines which are in danger of losing all their power: strangled by bad planning and management from the moment they leave the drawing board. This first, major, contract was set up a few years earlier by someone who had also landed on that faraway town: Mr Outward Bound! And it will take more than a little effort to clear up the mess.

Now John is not a metaphorical man, not one who looks to the heavens for his guiding stars; he works in the real world, the bricks-and-mortar one; he reads the newspapers and wears big boots. But this was a flash of lightning he found it impossible to ignore.

"I thought I'd best come and see what needs fixing," he said.

"Nothing needs fixing," I reply, with new-found calm. "Just for the moment, we are housed and watered and fed. Who could ever ask for more? But it's lovely to see you all the same."

We draw up contracts with other souls: of this much I am certain. We may agree to love one another, or even to abuse one another. We may contract to support and encourage each other or to kick each other awake. We stop at nothing in our quest as sentient beings to advance our own consciousness and that of our friends and our loves. We draw up our plans, separately and together, in some place of higher awareness before we descend into physical form and amnesia sets in; and then we take on our roles, we meet, and the play unfolds.

If all goes according to plan, we support one another in the jobs we've signed up to do; we help one another to complete our mission on earth. If indeed we have such a thing as a spiritual partner, this must be the purpose of such an arrangement, to expand each other beyond the limits of our previous horizons, beyond the smallness of our egoic realities, and into the authentic power and memories of our souls.

And with this powerful encounter, for both the parties concerned, comes a feeling of homecoming rather different from anything they have previously known. John, then, like me, has come home; furthermore, he's come to a road called after his namesake, St John: what an appropriate place for this husband-to-be to heal his own sore spots and re-ignite his power.

"Would that be John the Baptist or John the Apostle, this stream of Johns that have peopled your life?" asks my friend, as I recount this latest unlikely chapter. "Brother, uncles, teachers, friends..."

"Oh," I reply without a moment's hesitation, "St John the Apostle, of course."

Where did that come from? I've no idea.

27

New world

So we're held. Here is the recovery space of my dreams. Bodies mend, along with minds and hearts. What they need is time, and this is exactly the gift we've been given.

I may be out of a job, but no-one has a monopoly on colour and light, I remind myself. And it's grabbed me, this psycho-spiritual wand, this tool for lighting up hearts and souls. In one country after another, I've watched as lives that were dogged by heartbreak, abuse, loss, despondency or despair have been gently and steadily rebuilt. Over and over again, I've seen the light return to eyes dulled by pain and hopelessness. So I'd better find my own way to spread this tool and make it useful. But how? What is the mechanism, the tool, that will look after us as well as them? How, in a simple phrase, am I supposed to earn our keep?

The journalist meets the up-and-coming young composer.

"Ah yes," he says, twiddling his thumbs over his paunch. "The music man himself. What drives you to compose? What motivates, what *inspires* you to make such, er, *interesting* sounds?"

"The rent," says the composer.

Yes, well, I know the feeling. Ours, as it happens, is seen to for a good few months to come and I'm grateful down to my toes. But then what? My book has done well, it's true: 8000 copies sold in just a few months with a reprint due any day now; letters and emails from grateful readers. All of this has got to be good news: it means some kind of income, surely? Security, perhaps; in my wilder moments I dare to dream of a home, even – one to keep. But I've not reckoned on the publisher going bust and the royalties vanishing without trace.

"What?"

I was raised in a household that knew nothing of commerce; I was taught that we must work to serve our fellow man. It's an admirable principle, no-one can deny that, but not one, perhaps, which encourages one towards scrutiny of the motives of those who court us for business. It seems that I've embarked on a crash course in that basic skill.

We're here in the warmth, though; we're safe; we're living in love. It's the quiet after the storm: not a bad place to be. We're told that time does not exist in the land of the angels and gods; it's merely a mechanism that we've constructed for handling the business of life in a body. It certainly exists for us, then. Time is a good friend, too. Someone said that it's a device which stops everything from happening at once. We need this earthly device to integrate, to heal, to understand; to work it all out, one step at a time.

I'm here with my children and my mate and we'll find a way forward. I have to keep writing; it's another thing that's grabbed me. They asked Michelangelo how he created something as wonderful as David. David was there all the time, he said. All he had to do was find him, chip away at all the stone which obscured him from sight. I'm no Michelangelo, but we all need chisels. My chisels are words. I'll chip away, build up a client base, run a few workshops.

I shall start over; make my own world of colour; take light into the darker spaces; heal the world as I repair myself and those I love. Ah, and now three people have signed up for a course – well there's a start.

"Why does it work?" asks a student. "What's the mechanism? Wouldn't most people say that colour is too bland, too *ordinary*, to actually change anything?"

"It's a good question," I reply, "and there are quite a few answers to it, since light works on several levels all at once. How about this? Colour is the way that light expresses itself in the world that we know, and light is the building block of that world anyway. So there's nothing very bland at all about colour: it's one with the Source, really. It's extremely close to that mysterious something that gives rise to life itself."

There's silence, as the small handful of people in the room digest this thought.

"But the mechanism," this woman repeats. "What about the mechanism? *How* does it work? Why does it shift anything in your consciousness, if you plunge into a pink bath or spray your aura in gold?"

"Shame I can't source the pink bath or the gold spray," I'm thinking silently. "I need a product – one that I can trust."

But I carry on and answer the question.

"The quantum mechanics tell us that the universe consists of nothing but energy and information. That energy is actually light-energy. And to make *stuff*, matter – things, if you like, or us, come to that – then this light-energy lowers its vibration, slows down its movement, to a very low rate: so low, we don't even realize it's still moving. But in essence the things we can see and touch are still materialized from this energy, the energy of light. We – or our minds – forget this unlikely fact, but our bodies don't. Different colours are expressions of that light: in other words, they contain different information. That's why every culture on the planet shares much the same symbolism around colour: to see red or be green with envy or yellow-bellied or whatever, your only qualification is that you have to belong to the human race."

"Animals can be helped and healed by colour too," says another woman.

"Yes, they're sensitive to energy and respond well to colour when they're sick or in shock," I agree.

"But what we're doing here is using colour not just as an energy that heals you or makes you feel better than you did yesterday. We're talking about an energy that helps us to evolve, to become more fully aware of what we're doing with our lives; to see how we create what we create and how to change our reality if we'd rather have something better than we've known to date.

Recognize your *true colours* and you acknowledge something deep within yourself. You begin to reclaim the parts of yourself that you've given away. And then, you go further: you *use* the colours. That's when things really start to change: you sense the magnificence of who you are."

I'm on thin ice here. What these students have is the cards I've painted. Any kid could do it, but they won't deliver blue messages on to your skin or spray violet energy into your aura, to reinforce the impact of the words. For the moment, though, I'm safe – like me, they are interested by the ideas.

"So now we're getting to the why," I continue, "the how. Colour is the highest frequency in this world of matter that our senses can still get a hold of. Immerse yourself in that pink bath – use some natural food colouring, for instance – and your body picks up the information that's carried in the colour, and it decodes it, way faster and more deeply than your mind would ever do. It deciphers it. It uses this energy, absorbs it, metabolizes it, and then you get a shift: sometimes a small one; sometimes a bigger one. Sometimes it will ease a headache; other times it will mend a marriage."

"But what about the shadow?" asks the next person. "We know that green has all the expansiveness and generosity of nature, the open-mindedness and all the rest of it; but there's hatred and jealousy and all kinds of other stuff in there too. Coral is tender and empathetic but it can be a needy parasite."

"Sure," I agree. "We have to acknowledge the shadow, of course we do: naivete is never a powerful state of mind. But we have to befriend the dark places in ourselves and recognise their gifts, not judge them. Judge a terrorist and he'll shoot you. Love him and he'll most likely dissolve in tears – which is a good thing, because then you can start a conversation. Reclaiming the fuller picture of who we are, embracing our darkness, entering its warmth is a good thing: the shady bits start to dissolve; they yield up their gifts."

I can feel the atmosphere in the room growing a shade lighter already: there's just a hint of shoulders dropping; a whisper of air, as the breath moves in a fraction deeper.

"We change when we feel loved, not when we feel judged," I continue. "It's about seeing beyond the illusion, loving ourselves in spite of our fear. It's about looking into the darkness of what's hidden inside us and seeing its friendly warmth, its creative potential. Where would we be without the soil, or without our sleep – the place of all our dreams?"

"If Hitler had done that," says the first student, "instead of projecting his shadow at everyone else, the 1940s world would have looked a bit different."

Well that's for sure. The concepts have always got me going; always fired me up. It's easy to teach what we need to learn, to tell Hitler to love himself. How about loving our*selves*, though? How many of us come anywhere near to that? If we did, everyone would have perfect jobs, perfect homes, wonderful relationships, health; a perfect bank balance. We'd be flowing and abundant and thoroughly safe – all of us, including me.

I have no product, not one that I can any longer trust as a vehicle of the highest truth. A true colour remedy must contain the purest healing intention of its source. All the world, after all, is energy and information: the information, then, is contained within the energy of the product. So no, I have no product, no structure, no back-up, no corporate umbrella. I'm no longer teaching therapists, I'm merely sharing ideas. I'm Rapunzel, cast out into the wilderness, searching for a lost prince: for prince, read sovereignty, clarity, certainty, security, a grounded sense of identity and purpose.

But when Rapunzel had thought that she'd found her prince, she was stuck in the tower. Maybe I was stuck too, in someone else's structure, someone else's system, as I raced around the world; I was playing someone else's tune.

"How does it play out in practice, this language of colour?"

asks another keen student.

There are all kinds of answers to this question – enough to fill another volume at the very least. How about a book for lots of people, not just the abused, the dispossessed, the soul-searchers? I could take a leaf out of the magazine-creators' pages and make a book for popular consumption. The 'red' person at work, in love; red parents, red children; red symbols, red rooms, red flowers, remedies, gems, foods. The blue person; the pink person; the purple person, the yellow person. It will have beautiful pictures; it will fill the shelves of gift shops and the tables of waiting rooms. It will be a little like the books on star signs, but food for the senses too: visual and delicious. I shall call it *Colour Power*. The product? The essences and sprays? Never mind those for the moment – let's disseminate the information.

"Yes!" say the next publishers. "We love it. We'll do it at once."

And so they do. It's not so long before we have them in our hands, these shining books. Their vibrant images blaze; they reach out from every page, putting a smile on your face, setting your cells aglow with light and all the colours of the spectrum. For another few months, my colour world looks hopeful once again.

28

America

Three or four months later, that vibrant colourful book, full of beautiful pictures and the colour power that its title promised, has disappeared. Its publishers have shut the doors on an entire imprint, leaving several hundred authors stranded. Including me.

That wasn't it either, then: teaching, counselling, broadcasting – at home and abroad – book-making. What next? When one door shuts, another one slams in your face.

We're a few years down the road now from our grateful return to our home town. John is working to build up a business of his own, repairing broken contracts. He'd much rather work with me; he'd greatly prefer to make some small contribution in people's lives and hearts. Three houses have slid away from under our feet, as one landlord after another has decided to sell or to return home herself. House prices and rentals are soaring and funds are critically low. Our next move takes us to a student house in bedsit-land: heavy metal bands day and night; back lane strewn with used needles. This is not the life I prayed so hard to reclaim.

Besides, I'd thought that we each came in with a job to do: this is what my teachers and mentors have been telling me for years. Top marks for trying, surely? But does the divine Boss have a different opinion, I wonder, as my mate and I have another brain-storming session, racking our minds and fishing around for new ideas – and a new place to live.

Colour throws wonderful light on relationships: here's an aspect of the work that I love. So now I'm doing some work with couples; and the odd family here and there. *Make light work of relationships:* I like it. I set up a few seminars, work with a few clients, and before too much longer there's another book. We'll call it *Colour Talks*; people will see that growing happier doesn't have to hurt: they can have fun with their journeys through the looking glass.

But no-one else will get to publish it this time. No, we shall take the thin remains of my legacy and do the thing ourselves: the best designers, the best printers, the best intentions. Here at last is a product that won't go away: we can hold my latest offerings in our hands, thousands of them.

Or we can ship them to America. We're in love, my husband and I: we're in love with the New World. We've been to the East Coast for a few scattered workshops, but it's the West Coast that has taken hold of our hearts.

Our fairy godmother, Cousin Patricia of the school fees, has an old place there that she doesn't use too often. It has a roof of a kind – one that leaks, with half of it falling down. We can use it whenever we like and will we please repair the place a little? We're only too happy to do so: a leaking roof – or half of one – is a whole lot better than none.

Well now we've been there several times already. There's something strange that seems to happen when I'm there. I sense a presence in the house: it's friendly and warm. I can't see it or touch it, but I can feel it; sometimes I hear it – especially when I'm writing. This wise and benevolent energy seems to flow right through my pen. I don't know its name: I suspect it's an ancestor or maybe it's an angel. It hardly matters anyway.

"They're all airheads in California," say my friends from the old days. "You're catching the bug."

If this is the natural home of airheads, it suits me well; I've never felt so much at home anywhere on the planet. And now I'm headed towards that coast once more, to Los Angeles, and it's a long time since I've been filled with such exhilaration and hope. My long years of knocking on doors are finally bearing fruit: I've been invited to appear on US television. This is a major network and the programme is for early evening: maximum number of viewers. God *is* in his heaven after all.

So we've shipped those new books to New York and they'll do the rest of the journey overland. We'll have them there in time for the broadcast, which is scheduled for the 12th of September 2001: CBS, prime-time; and these slots don't come easy.

Yes! What a relief. I'm out there again at last, doing my mission, more broadcasts to follow. There are people to talk to who will listen and enjoy it; seminars booked for later. After the programme when all the calls come in, I shall team up with friends: package by night and post by day; we'll send books out by the cartload. So I'd better get ready. I'm booked in to one of those nice airport hotels so I can sleep off the jetlag.

I'm half-snoozing when the mini-earthquake comes and shakes me awake: no Buddha beside me here, keeping me safe. Tinkle tinkle, goes the breaking glass; shudder shudder, goes my bed. I abandon my shut-eye and get stuck into the novel I didn't finish on the plane. Sleep comes eventually; now it's pitch black and I'm down deep. So when the screech of the alarm shatters every nerve in my body, I can't work out where I am. I fumble for the light: where's my bag, my passport? What shall I wear?

Oh yes, of course, it means *fire*, doesn't it. You're not supposed to get nicely dressed up for the furnace; you're meant to leg it down the stairs. If I must, then, I'll join the troops in the hall. The staff are weary too. Now they're saying it's a false alarm, but can they figure out how to turn the thing off? It screeches at full pelt for 20 minutes until someone cracks the stop code, and we all stagger back to our beds. I wake the next morning to find my favourite ring – the lovely garnet one I've worn every day for 25 years – bent right out of shape; it won't even fit on my finger. I begin to wonder if this was a false alarm after all. Something is up and it doesn't feel like a good thing. So I go to my friend Tiffany who's expecting me: she set the broadcast up, she's a proper ally in a storm. It will be much quieter and gentler in her welcoming home. And so it is, until seven o'clock next morning, the 11th of September, and Tiffany comes through to where I'm sleeping:

"John's on the phone, tearing his hair out. He's asked us to turn on the TV."

We yawn, stretch and tune in to horrors beyond anyone's wildest, sickest nightmares. I've never been to New York; it's not hit my personal radar before. It's a while before I even begin to absorb what's going on. This is something like a horror film but I don't watch horror so I can't really grasp it at all. That's the thing with shock: it makes you dumb. We sit there, stroking the dog, drinking tea. And we can't do a damn thing. We can't go to New York or Washington to make ourselves useful: the airports are shut down. Which means I can't go home either: the ports are all closed. I'll stay on with Tiffany a while; she needs company now.

What about my books, I wonder – those precious objects into which I have sunk all my remaining funds? They arrived in New York yesterday, all 3000 of them: a day after me, a day before the bombs. How will I get hold of them now, and what will I do with them when I've got them?

"They'll be in the port," says Tiffany, "but the office that deals with them – that's another matter. It may well have gone down with the rubble."

In this stark new context of life and death, it's obscene to be even thinking about something as trivial as books. Love and bright lights, rainbows and psycho-spiritual counselling: this is hardly the stuff that America wants now. There are bodies out there, broken and bleeding or dead; lives thrown right into the middle of hell. The subject today is war. The image of *The Tower*, from the myths embodied in the ancient wisdom system of the Tarot, stares us in the face daily: bodies falling from a castle stronghold in collapse; the dissolution of the old order; the crumbling of structures – armaments and wealth – that have stood as markers of temporal wealth and power. The Tarot says this image indicates the making way – dare I even think it in a world of such excruciating pain? – for some new kind of order.

But eventually I *must* move on: I can't just sit here, murmuring "how awful," waiting for the Phoenix to rise from the proverbial ashes. So I meander up the coast to the house with the mended roof, and I sit there instead. I can't sit for long, though: I'm getting jittery. John is about to drive my children 50 miles to a family party in a peaceful spot in the South of England and panic is gripping me by the throat. Will I ever see them again, *any* of them? I'm shaking; it's ridiculous. I take a quick look at myself behaving in this odd fashion and then it's suddenly obvious what is going on.

We do this all the time. Our bodies pick up on what other people are feeling. Spend time around a depressed person and you'll soon feel worn out. Spend time around a natural comedian and your energy will expand and spread like sunshine. Here are tens of thousands of people all over America in deep trauma. Will they ever see their loved ones again? It's a huge, burning, terrifying question: no wonder the rest of us are in panic. We're all part of the same field of energy, after all; we're all one stuff.

Then a strange remedy comes in for me. John has suggested back in the spring that I write a book about Dorothy Gale and her Yellow Brick Road. He's urged me to. I've started and stopped a time or two. But now, all of a sudden, feelings and ideas around it come pouring in.

I don't know much about what's happening out there, but one thing is clear: this madness is coming from deep darkness and fear, the recurring story of life on this planet. Just for the moment, this sudden apocalypse feels like the end of civilisation as we've known it. Out there in New York and Washington, it's a living hell; the fear in other cities is at fever pitch. But here, in this old house in a remote spot three thousand miles from all that horror, there are angels. I'm beginning to feel oddly safe in spite of everything.

That child-heroine, Dorothy, lived on a fear-planet too: it was called Kansas City. No-one was particularly happy, no-one laughed or did very much about love, and no-one really heard anyone else – not from their hearts. The bottom line was that nobody even knew themselves: not Dorothy, nor anyone else. For that to happen, in order to find out who she was, this brave kid had to find her way to Oz. And here, once she had reached the place by courtesy of a cyclone – not unlike the whirlwind that hit those American cities in real time – everything broke out from the dull grey monotone where nobody could see with any clarity at all, into a new reality where people dared to open their hearts, to show their true colours, to be themselves. They *talked* to each other, for heaven's sake. They even listened.

The airports are open again now but I'm scribbling. Sometimes I want to fly back to England; I'm missing my family. But, "Please don't," says John. "Please keep on writing. We're OK here. We'll see you soon."

Maybe there's something here worth exploring. *Follow Your Yellow Brick Road*, I'm calling it. There seem to be some helpful clues hidden inside this little fairy tale: I'm enjoying the exploration. It's just another little piece of the puzzle, another step on the way, but it feels oddly relevant. Dorothy is everyman, everywoman: she's looking for something. She says it's home that she's seeking; it would be nearer the mark to call it self-responsibility; or perhaps it's called growing up. Whatever you call it, she's on a journey with a destination. This trek will direct her away from the search outside herself, where she's searching for a wizard who will hand her the answers and sort out her problems, and towards the inside, to the place where she will find God, or her higher power, or whatever name you may wish to give to the Mind behind the Universe or the Creative Power within ourselves.

Seven whole weeks have passed at last. I've been writing around the clock and I'm stiff as a board from head to foot, I can scarcely walk, but something feels complete.

America is in deep shock: the ground on which its commercial engine-house has long stood is a ghost town, a pile of rubble that has gradually faded from a screaming inferno to a whisper of ruination.

But magically, miraculously, in the thick of this collapse that has shattered lives and hearts, my friend Diantha has gathered up a group of people who want to *know* this stuff I've been exploring. They're even prepared to face the aeroplanes again for this little seminar: these determined travellers have sensed that light holds some of the deepest clues for us all. They know that we're in this together, that myth and fairy tale remain with us through the ages for the simple reason that they're the story of humanity itself.

So I'm invited to go and meet them anyway. I touch down in Chicago as the last sentences are complete: it's only a first draft, this Oz-based offering, but it will do for a workshop. And the next four days are a riot: we've never had so much fun in our lives. Diantha's a star.

So is Dorothy, as she deals with the forces of darkness and interprets the hopeful hints offered by the light. Maybe we should all take a leaf out of her book.

29

The dream

I'm back in England. The leaves are falling fast. There's a spiritual harvest on offer too: a group that meets for Satsang once a month, somewhere nearby. I'm not too sure what the word means but I go along anyway: I know there will be meditation, some discussion, some soul-food. As I'm leaving, I find myself talking to Desmond, my host, about Magdalen.

I'm still holding the vision – that one about changing the past – but the daily reality of her life is unrelenting. She contains so much, this child of mine. Other children have made fun of her and mocked her in the cruellest ways imaginable; teachers have bullied her, smashed her frail confidence to smithereens. It's easy: dump your stuff on the person who's least able to fight back. It's only the story of humankind in all its fear, after all. But I see the loneliness behind her eyes; I feel it, whether I'm beside her or away. It's in every cell of her body, like an east wind, penetrating all the hidden places.

Desmond follows me to the hall at the end of the Satsang. He looks into my eyes and says, "Yes, but all that can be changed. You will reach the point where the accident never happened."

What? Can I be hearing him right? These are the words that came to me in the funfair – nine years ago, ten? I've never spoken them to a single soul; not even my husband; not even my kids. I fling my arms around this man, I thank him for his vision and I go on my way.

"We can change the past. It has to be true."

This certain, sure conviction is coming from somewhere deep inside me. It's coming from a place that knows.

"But you mustn't worry, Mum," Magdalen says a day or two later as we're talking about a recent scene at school. "Really. I don't believe them, you see. They say those things and I'm like 'well, you're wrong; you don't know what you're talking about'. It's like I'm not there; it's like I'm watching someone else and I know all those things they're saying have nothing to do with me."

She's out of her body so much of the time. Maybe it's just as well. Maybe that's how it's done – the slow recovery, the staying sane in spite of it all. The search for miracle-workers around the planet has yielded steady rewards. Her ongoing cranial treatment has certainly helped: there are fewer headaches, less abdominal pain. The limp is as bad as ever, though, and walking's a slog. Her foot will hardly let a shoe on; it's stiff as a board, her ankle is like wood – and still the foot is cramping around the clock. Sometimes her hand and fingers are too. Those are the times when it's difficult to write or hold a spoon.

She has a new friend, though. He's called Kim and he's old enough to be her father. He is a father, in fact: he has four glorious children of his own. One of them has a mind like Einstein and a heart like Gandhi, but his hip is crumbling all away and he's in pain around the clock. Kim gets it: he knows how she feels. He's a consultant physician but he's lost all his professional marbles, as he puts it, to do something else. The something else? You guessed it: he's a healer, world class.

He has invited me on a course with another doctor, a gentle giant of an Indian mystic.

"You come along too," he tells Magdalen. "You can help Bee with the kids and make the tea."

So they've got her on the table, these two doctors, and they're doing weird and wacky things. One of them is at her head, the other at her feet. And all of a sudden, for the first time in ten years, she can feel her foot. For a second or two, she even wiggles a toe.

"It was the pelvis that took the smash first," Kim says. "Not the head; that was next. The main impact, the shock, the memory of the event, is held in her pelvis: it's completely blocking the traffic."

Magdalen is crying now. She's not done that before: more my speciality than hers. She's crying because she can see a beam of light at the end of the tunnel. They talk all night through, she and Kim. Now she's crying some more: it's a heaving, sobbing cry of desperation from a heart that's battered, bruised and alone. "Nobody gets it, nobody cares," she sobs. "It's just me and Mum. That's all it's ever been."

"No, but they will," says Kim. "They will. There don't have to be too many that get it; often one or two are enough. And one day you will meet that special person: *he* will get it *completely*. Just you wait."

And then comes the dream. I'm in a café with Magdalen beside me. Louise Hay is serving us with tea and cakes. Catching sight of Magdalen, she beckons us through to another room of this little establishment. It's a flower shop with just one long table, piled high with white lilies more beautiful than anything you've seen in your life: thick, lush, snow-white blooms bursting with divine scent. Louise hands me a single stalk, covered in thick, rich blossoms, and tells me that this is the promise that the 100% healing we've sought all these years will manifest, and it will be soon. We return with her to the land of tea and cakes, and Marianne Williamson enters the room, filling the entire space with energy: a return to love.

I wake up in shock. I need time to process this vision: I'll walk into Oxford; find a café. As I walk, I feel a cosmic breeze, the grace that filled this dream: it rushes on through me and out of me and brushes everything in sight. The walls, the trees, the bicycles, the people: their lives will surely never be quite the same again. Nothing can remain unmoved by this holy spirit, this love that's pervading leaf and cell.

Both of these authors teach the radical power of love over fear. And flowers? They do so many things. They are nature's great and ever-renewing gift. They can be used to make subtle, potent remedies, too: the lily is the one for the wounded healer.

Well my child and I are wounded healers all right. But nothing like as wounded as we were. Watch out, world: the phoenix is rising out of that infernal ash.

And now we're in Dublin, because the dream has kick-started a new process. People are showing up from nowhere. This Dublin healer that we're visiting has a reputation for stimulating damaged nerves to grow again. Yes he's done a little something; I do believe there's been a little shift. We'll go there a few more times before we're done: who would stay away from that chocolate shop, anyway?

But now comes the big one. We're in London, visiting Carlo. We've been told he's a wiz at taking shocks and traumas out of the body memory, and he's just finished her first session. It's eleven years since her accident, almost to the day.

"Go carefully for a day or two," he says. "You'll probably feel shaky for a while."

She's feeling very strange indeed. She's fighting back the tears. Next stop Starbucks. That'll be a hot chocolate, thanks. Yes please, the froth, the foam, the cream, the works. Oh and biscotti, lots of them – smothered in chocolate. (It's a great homoeopathic, chocolate: it does wonders for someone needing a shot of love. Right now, though, we're not doing the homoeopathic doses that will waft a little flavour-free invisible stuff into our auras or our cells. No thanks – we'll stay at the chunky end of the scale.)

And now we're home again and I'm tucking my precious child safely into her bed with hot water bottles filling every nook and cranny. She's ice-cold, shaking from head to toe. It carries on all night, this violent tremor. But next evening, we're all together: the three siblings, and me, and John. It's rare enough, these days, with universities and jobs. We're sharing a family meal and something is completely different. Magdalen is present; she's *here*. She listens, she speaks, she's right in there with the chat. She laughs and smiles. And yes thanks, she'll have more of that chocolate-and-chilli stuff, it's quite delicious.

She's going to start feeling things again, and it won't all be pleasant. She'll start to feel the fear of passing cars; she'll get flashes where all of a sudden she has been hit on the head; she will cry. But she's back in her body: this has got to be the start of a level of healing she has never reached before.

You can't heal even a sore toe if you're not around to partake in the process. It's only when we're in our bodies that we can do life at all.

30

Dolphins

It was a long time ago, that promise I made. It's what my child longed for from the first time those friendly sea-mammals gazed out at her from our television screen – long before she hit intensive care.

"Come back to us, stay with us," I said to her as she lay in her hospital bed, "and one day – when I can – I'll take you to swim with the dolphins."

She's read books about dolphins since then; she's talked to people about something called Human Dolphin Therapy. She's patiently waited, and she knows there's something here for her. And now it's eleven years on from that day in the hospital and my friend Ellen is lodged in paradise: she's in Hawaii, on the big island, camping on the beach.

"Sure, I'll find you a place to stay," she says.

But a week later she adds another clause:

"Come on a colour course. I've met a new system – it's *amazing*."

No thanks. Been there done that. Learned it, practised it, taught it; tried everything; had it up to the ears; been cleaned out big time. It's something else, thanks, whatever it is that I'm seeking. Enjoy the course, though – I'm sure you'll find some great students.

"*Pleeeease*." She needs students; she's got to make it happen. Pleeease.

I don't want this; I'm miffed. The place she's directed us to is far from cheap and this will be only the second holiday Magdalen has had in her life. I'm so over anything that calls itself colour therapy, she can't even begin to imagine.

"But you're still writing books about it:" very annoying, this pesky voice, this elbow, digging me in the ribs right from the inside.

"So? We all have to do *some*thing."

I'm fond of my friend and – well, she's found us somewhere to stay, I guess. Oh well, I sigh, OK then, if you really must – but only for the moments when my child is cramming for exams. We're there to play, right? We're after sun, sea, dragon fruits; plumeria blossoms for our hair. We're not coming all that way to *work*.

A week later: "Hey, how about we hold the course on your balcony?"

"*I beg your pardon?* You've got to be joking. On our lovely balcony? The one we've waited for all these years? The one that's busted my brand new credit card? We've waited all this time, we're putting everything we can borrow into this holiday-of-a-lifetime – and you want to fill our space with floaty people."

"I love Ellen," says Magdalen. "Let her do it. We'll be out all day anyway."

"Oh all right then, come and disturb our beautiful peace. Fill our ocean view with strangers and munch away at our precious time. We'll find ways to escape, though, you bet we will. We'll run down to the beach. You can work all you like."

"Thanks!"

So here we are, in tropical paradise, right out in the vastest ocean mass the planet has ever seen. The place panders to every preconception that images of the South Pacific have ever planted in your mind's eye: the flowers grown in heaven, the air sweet and moist, the greenery thick, sensuous, lush; the water so blue and turquoise it must be a joke – an optical illusion laid on to make you think it's real. It's so hot I could faint.

"You'll meet Melissie in the morning," Ellen says. "I'll put the bottles out tonight, so they're ready for class tomorrow."

The jetlag soon kicks in and we sink into a hot slumber in our soft beds, a gentle breeze wafting through the raffia-filled spaces where windows would be at home. I'm deeply asleep now, and

I'm dreaming: there's a round bottle right in front of my eyes and it's holding a strange combination of colours – deep magenta over transparent white. This is one of those full-colour dreams that take you over completely; they seem to go on all night.

"I must ask this Melissie person to make that nice concoction when I meet her," I tell myself as I awaken.

I'm yawning and stretching and I can't get the magenta-and-white image out of my mind. But it's time for breakfast. There's fruit juice in the fridge – and mangoes, papayas, pineapples. Let's get to it.

I open my bedroom door on to the balcony with the breath-taking ocean panorama spread out beyond it in the early morning light. Staring me in the face much closer than this, just a few feet in front of my face, is the bottle of my last night's dream: same configuration, same tone, same feel. She's there already, this Melissie. She's ahead of the game.

I pick up the gentle, rounded bottle and feel it: right now I could drink that nectar inside it. I look at the number on its lid. Funny, that – it's number 11: that just happens to be the number of my birth. You can change your other numbers simply by changing your name, but you can't change the year, the month, the day that you were born. Your birth number is fixed; it tells you stuff about your destiny, about what you're here to do.

Yes, well – let's go play with the dolphins. We've got our flippers and our boards. We've got the goggles too. Hey Ellen – show us what to do! The waves crash against the black volcanic rocks that seem to erupt everywhere on this coast: how are we supposed to flip-flop our way out there without being beaten to a pulp? But they've slithered away already, these girls. They're like dolphins. Magdalen is way ahead of me with Ellen right beside her; she's gliding over these tropical waters as though she's lived here all her life.

I make it through the beating foam eventually, and follow my leaders. I'm gazing into the magical scene below. There's coral here, in every rainbow hue; fish in stripy jackets, bright yellow and black; and golden ones, royal blue, and pink. There are sea flowers, waving their fronds in the gentle currents beneath.

"What about the sharks?" I've asked Ellen earlier on, more than a little anxious.

I'm a beginner in this game of trust. There are predators out there and I know it: the shadow is lurking there, in the depths. How do you ever know what's below you, behind you?

"They say the sharks don't come where the dolphins are," she's replied. "And the dolphins are here almost every day."

So I've entrusted my last-born to her dolphin sister; she's in heaven. And now here they are, a whole pod! They're circling below us, soundless and mystical; but their sonar reaches us anyway. We'll know that later, because we'll find it's changed the way we feel. Ellen wiggles her body like a mermaid as she dives deep to join her grey friends with their great long noses. Time is suspended in the magical silence of this place.

The dolphins stay with us, dancing, playing; from time to time we catch a note of their clicking song. They go off a little distance, but soon they're back again. From time to time, one of them will come so close you can stretch an arm and touch its back. Eventually, they move on: enough for today. It's a long way back to shore. I fight the breaking waves as I flip-flop my way through the sand and the rocks, clumsy as a seal on mud. I'm ready for lunch. Melissie has arrived: she's come all the way from Africa. It's time for the first afternoon's class. OK then, I'll join them for a while.

Have I heard it all before? Ah no, I have not – not at all. It's on a new level, this system, I can't deny it. This is wisdom that Melissie is bringing to us as she speaks: powerful and authentic. I'm not exactly hooked, not yet – but I have to confess that in spite of myself I'm more than a little intrigued. She has called this method Colourworks.

"Because colour works," she says quietly to me later. "Doesn't it?"

"Yeah right," I'm thinking, "maybe it does, for people with lives – people with homes, a bank balance, the stuff that goes with it."

But I'm silent. No-one here knows the relentlessness of the path I've tried so many ways to escape. They don't know that the philosopher's stone I've sought for so long feels as far away as it felt the day I lost my job; that my chisels feel as blunt as wooden spoons. No, they see me as the person who's done the work, taught the people, written the books. I'm the one with the answers. And so, of course, is she.

"What did you do?" Melissie asks me later, "before you got weird?"

Ah, life before weird: that was another lifetime; I scarcely remember.

"A bit of this and that," I reply. "Hung out in Kansas City. Chopped wood, you know, carried water: that kind of thing."

We're reminiscing about the past now, the times we spent in England, and in Egypt, on a boat, learning about our shared tool – nearly meeting properly but somehow never quite. We're beginning to find that we have trodden paths that are eerily similar, especially these recent years. Not so much at the very beginning: she has spent a childhood in the African bush; she's had baby hippopotami around the Kenyan kitchen table. I've had the English city centres with tickets to the shows.

"I'd love to go on safari; it must be *fascinating*."

"Boring," says Melissie. "I'll take your seat in the Stalls."

I tell her about my dream, and my intention to commission the bottle that I find she's already made.

"Oh yes, that's the Metatron bottle," she says.

I wouldn't know about that. I like the colour though; that mysterious mixture has worked its way into my blood. Yes, it's good, this system she's pulled through from somewhere, downloaded into the world – it's very good. I'm watching her work and I'll support her if I can.

Right now, though, it's party time. We're a band of floaty people all together. We're floating with the dolphins in the sun. We're travelling down to the great volcano; we're walking in the sacred gardens, watching the dragonflies hover and the turtles dive. Magdalen and I are glad we shared our lanai: how dull it would have been all on our own.

"How would you like to contribute to the growth of Colourworks?" Ellen asks each of us as the teaching winds up.

"I could write a book, I suppose," I suggest, a little vaguely.

Yes, I could do that, some time, somewhere; but not yet. I'm still pacing my way along that yellow brick road. My time is fully taken up.

Magdalen is deeply peaceful as she reads. The tedious set text of her war novel is softened by the lush tropical sun that beats down on our lanai from dawn till dusk. She likes the colours too, and all the floaty people – she's grown up around these. It's where she feels at home.

But she talks to Melissie all the same – about the less peaceful parts: her school life, her learning struggles, her cramping, dragging foot; the isolation, the taunting, the relentlessness of it all. She's the Tin Woodman, Dorothy's friend: she's all about love, but it feels as if the Wicked Witch – otherwise known as 'life as she has experienced it' – came to call and took away a part of her self. She's felt broken and crushed: will she ever re-gather herself?

Her wizards have done wonders for her, it's true. So much of her is better than it was, thanks to Carlo the Great: that's what we call him, our wizard in London (what do you bet we knew *him* in Rome?). He's the one who puts lives back together again; he takes out the shock; he re-unites the body with the soul. We visit him regularly; he's unlocking the pieces of her that got shut away; he's bringing back to life the crushed parts of her *heart*, let alone her brain, hips, foot, you name it – but there's still a way to go.

"You'll let go of it when you say yes to it," Melissie tells her.

Now here's a clue. Maybe the way we change the past is to change the thought we have about the past. Maybe the task we face in our journeys is to dissolve our judgments. Because when we do the thing that we all do, categorizing and labelling and putting our experience (or that of other people) into boxes that we believe we can handle or understand, what we are really doing is hardening it, contracting it down. In this process of condensation, the thing – whatever it is – will lose its fluidity, its connection to the Allness, its own capacity to grow us and expand us beyond our previous constraints.

What's more, when we judge something, whether the judgment is directed towards an event, or a behaviour, or anything at all, what we do is to separate ourselves further from the Oneness that is our salvation. "You can't fight it right," says this new friend, "you can only love it right." The truth of this is self-evident, after all: we all change when we feel loved; this goes for a bashed-up foot or a bashed-up life, it's all the same. But living this truth: ah, here's the challenge.

And then there's Aka, a master in the ancient healing arts of Huna. She's long since been dispossessed, like so many of her countrymen and women. She lives as they do – on the beach. And she's full of magic: she calls in the dolphins on her mystical, home-fashioned flute. We watch them respond to her call, whooping and leaping. What are they telling us? Why are they jumping so much? Maybe they remember something we've forgotten: maybe they're reminding us that life is a celebration, a party, a ball.

"You've been given a gift," Aka tells my child. "It wasn't an accident but a great, rare gift. It's what has made you and will grow you into the life you are meant to lead. You must embrace your calling, your destiny: you have work to do. I recognize you – because I see myself in you. Never give up hope."

So maybe the wicked witch, or Life, didn't take something away after all – from Magdalen, from Aka, from any of us who have been deconstructed and reconstructed. Maybe, rather than have something vital removed, Life took the opportunity to pour in something extra.

Ellen, Melissie, Aka; we love you all. And all the dolphins too. And we must leave you. We're on our way home now. We're filled up, on friendship and tropical air; on colour and renewed faith; on food of every description. And dolphins: they've entered our lives and they're there to stay.

There's something about being within arm's length of those creatures, guests in their home territory, that's awesome, in the original sense of that word. It's holy; it's sacred. This is not something you can describe, but I'd even dare to say that being around these gentle cetaceans changes your life.

"You know the dolphins?" says Magdalen, as the plane floats peacefully above the clouds. "They filled my body with joy. I felt it all inside. I'd forgotten what that felt like. I'm beginning to feel alive again – properly alive."

31

Colourworks

I made a promise, though – and another year has passed. It's time for the next project to begin. I'm writing: words for websites, words for books. Words words words. They chip and shape, they penetrate and rub. They scour away at the surface of things and little by little, they take me to a world beyond themselves – a wordless, silent place of truth, of beauty even. They show me what I need to see and feel; they remind me what I know.

I've promised Melissie some words too, and that means Africa. Perhaps here the task of these words will be different: maybe they will do the reverse of the construction attempt that I'm engaged in. Maybe I'm offering Melissie something a little more like the process of eating that Japanese meal: looking at her works of art and dissecting them piece by piece.

This set of gems that Melissie has made – the oils, the herbal waters, the sprays with all kinds of names and colours – have healing jobs to do. If we're to do a useful job here, making a book, we must return the pieces to their palette, to offer them up for digestion by those who will put them to good use.

So here we are, sitting in the sun. Table Mountain reaches up to heaven, in the blazing blue beyond us. It's inviting the archangels to lunch. The root chakra of the planet, they call it: the energy generator that fuels all the rest. Maybe so: Africa is passion and ferocity and love; it has the earthy, grinding presence of a great motor; it can flow and swell and rise, or it can seize up with the sheer enormity of itself. It does nothing by halves and everything by extremes. There are no compromises in this feverish continent: it's unequivocal in every way. We're sitting in the bay, munching my favourite foods.

"It happens here," Melissie has reminded me, 18 months

before this, as I've listened to her teaching in Hawaii.

My mind had glimpsed this already. We've checked out the skies and drawn a blank. No heaven out there. We've checked out the past and found that on the whole it's quite a grizzly place. We've checked out the future, as best we can: in general it is full of fear; there's not much else about it that we know. The conclusion is obvious: we must check *in* – here. Where else is there?

Dorothy searched the universe for heaven before she found it in her own backyard. We do much the same as she did; the question is whether we make it as far as our backyards.

Yes, my mind has known all that. My body has still held back; it doesn't feel safe. Not yet.

"Maybe when I find something that works," I'm thinking. "Seminars, books that spread their wings and reward me for the effort. Maybe when I see that the pain behind Magdalen's eyes has turned into light that stays the course – the light of safety and confidence, not just the Trojan pretence of it to make the rest of us feel OK. Maybe when I can afford the food, the rent, when *something* grounds itself; when some kind of security arrives, for keeps. I'm not asking for a whole lot: certainty; security; a steady sense of fruitfulness and purpose."

But more and more, my cells are gaining their faith. Let's take back our power, draw back the curtains, invite heaven in – right here, right now. There's nowhere else for it to be; no other time-frame either.

I strongly suspect this means we must open our hearts.

That's quite easy to do, sitting here in the blazing warmth, mountains on one side, open sea the other. We drive around the ocean road, sipping coffee, looking for gemstones as we go. It's a gem itself, this small city – one of the most beautiful places on earth.

Twin souls, twin flames? She's my twin *sister*, this woman. We think alike, we feel alike, we laugh at the same things. We've been raised on different ends of the planet but they must have used the same culture to feed us on.

"Colour reminds us how simple the whole thing is, if we allow it to be," says Melissie.

Simple, perhaps, but not bland. No. It's the very opposite. I'm here, equipped with my recording tapes and my scribbling pad. I'm conscientious to the last. We shall chat away and the trusty machine will record every word, then I shall unscramble it and reconstruct it into something simple and straightforward, which people can read. Easy!

The real agenda, though, seems to be something else. In my innocence, I've signed up for total immersion in the magical energies of the colourful concoctions that Melissie and Africa have been dreaming up for years.

So here we are now, on the southernmost tip of Africa, next stop Antarctic. The whales are still here but not for long; they will take their new youngsters and swim south for the winter feed. Not me though – no thanks, whales, you go have all the cold you like, I'm done with all of that.

The sun beats down on our arms and faces in the most friendly way as we stroll through the village. The jacaranda is in full bloom; the frangipani fills the air with rose-and-jasmine scent. Those perfumes are the king and queen of all the natural essences in the world, delivered through the air and straight into our senses.

"They call the soul mates in, those flowers," someone told me years ago.

Well thanks, you luscious blooms, I think you did that already. Do you call in the angels too? You're angels of a kind yourselves, you flowers, gently descended into the world we know and understand.

I'm delving into Colourworks. I've loved these rounded coloured gems from soon after I set eyes on them on the Hawaiian lanai, glinting and winking in the light. It was not only the deep magenta bottle that grabbed me, the one I'd dreamed of, but the others – especially the ones rich in copper-brown, the ones I needed if I was to land myself firmly on this rich brown planet. The colour combinations are earthy, fruity; they're good enough to eat or drink. They're not for internal consumption, of course, so I do the next best thing, the thing Melissie recommends: choose a bottle, run a bath and pour the whole lot in. If there's a Jacuzzi handy, so much the better.

As it happens, there is. I'm lying here and the foamy colours are belting me, beating me up from head to toe. My body can't deny they're there; it can't resist or ignore the impact of these colours, the carriers of information from the highest light, so it doesn't even try. At first the water is chocolate brown. At the end, it's turned clear. Where did all that colour go? It must have gone into me! My skin has drunk them deep; maybe they're travelling to where they're needed most. OK then, time for supper. Let's go to the beach!

I'm staggering out of the bath. I'm lead; I'm bricks. It looks like there's been a change of plan. I crawl into bed and sleep for 14 hours.

So much for the floaty person. No more, no more; she'll never fly again.

"Or will you?" says Melissie. "That was the heaven on earth bottle. Heaven is here on earth; we're agreed on that. But earth's in heaven too. You can be wherever you like, but you have to be here first. You have to be in a body."

Yes, I know: I've been getting it, all these years – slowly, but steadily. It's the body that *knows*. How can it be that bathing in these subtle remedies can have such radical effects?

"You know how, and why," says Melissie. "You've already taught thousands of other people much of what they know about the way it works."

Other people, yes... I've believed it, too, as I've watched their lives transform. The memories, the traumas, the story: all these are held in the body; but the wisdom is in there too. Bodies are deeply wise; our minds may reject the gifts that colour brings, but our bodies accept them every time. It's the body that decodes the crucial information carried on the wings of light. I've explained this quite lucidly in the past, with conviction and faith – to other people. It's *my* body, or perhaps my mind, in the wake of one betrayal after the next, that has hesitated to believe and receive; my heart that has needed to be convinced. Well this body, this heart, has landed with a thump; this floaty person has zoomed right in to earth.

We chat; I learn; I record; I make notes. The bottles are affecting me in all kinds of ways. My body feels stronger and my dreams are a riot. Strange and new information reveals itself to me through these feisty baths, and through the days and the nights.

It's time now to bathe in the bottle of my Hawaiian dream: that strange concoction of inner light shrouded by the deep darkness of magenta above. Melissie said it had to do with Metatron, that Archangel of whom I know so little. But I'm on overload already: I'm tuned out, not in. Who is Metatron, anyway? I don't even think to ask. And I'm a little hesitant to plunge into this odd-looking mixture, this strange cocktail of light and dark, even in spite of my dream – but I do it anyway.

All kinds of things unfold in its wake: not least, a vivid dream of loss and renewal – my father is here, and an ancient figure called Melchisedek. I'm told he will restore to us everything that has been lost. But I don't know who Melchisedek is, so I ask my friend.

"Ah," says Melissie, "The last Priest King, and the head of the line that came down through to Moses and then to Christ. You and I are part of that line: we've come through Christianity. I've worked with the energies of Melchisedek ever since Colourworks was born."

I don't know how she pours these divine energies into her

magical recipes, nor do I need to: I suspect it has to do with a quality of being rather than anything that she particularly does. But I'm living and breathing Colourworks, I'm finding that indeed it works. My friend has created something beautiful and miraculous. There are people coming to her from far and wide; they're suffering from cancer, or full-blown AIDS, and they go away changed: sometimes the AIDS has vanished clean away. Unexplained and wonderful things are happening here; I will make a book with all my heart.

"Will you come with me to Boston in the spring?" asks Melissie. "I really need you there."

You bet I will. And have a book all ready too. We'll hit America; no bombs can stop us this time. And while we're at it, let's go play in California.

"Good idea," says Melissie. "You're always busy. Something, someone, has to make you stop."

So here we are, six months later, in the Californian spring. We're all there together: my husband, my daughter, my friend. This place has all the peace you can dream of, but the restlessness is still there. I have work to do, things to teach. And here's one house we shan't be thrown out of – if only the US red tape department would let us in. What exactly is it, this work? What is it that's been blocking the doors, or slamming them in my face? I *must* make something happen! I want a home. I need a job. I want to sink my roots in deep somewhere. Here?

The rainy season has been a long one, but it's drier now. The sun is out; the leaves are gleaming. I'm running back from town; I'm happy, excited: a good friend is coming to call. He'll help us get working in America, I'm sure he will; he knows all kinds of stuff. I'm nipping down the jagged stone steps towards the house, but I've failed to notice that through the long wet season that preceded our visit, their ancient moss has turned to mould and they're like black ice. The next thing I know, both my feet have slipped from under me and I'm flying through the air. Crash! I've landed horizontally and I'm screaming. Nicola is standing over me, reaching out her hand. She's stunned and mute.

I wriggle my toes and feet, and carefully try lifting my legs a little: they move! It'll be OK. John has heard the screams and come running; together, they help me into the house.

"Two spinal fractures," says the doctor. "A major one here, behind the heart; one here at the kidneys – that one's less acute."

So I'm grounded. And bewildered, because I thought I was done with all of that. I thought my messages were positive and upbeat – the kind that create *good* stuff. I thought I had been trusting, like they told me to. I've been trying so *hard* to let go. There must be something I've been missing.

"You can't *try* to let go," says an annoying little voice inside. "That's what's called a contradiction in terms. Letting go is something you do, or you don't."

"I get the idea," says another part of me, "but – owww! – trusting it, that's the hard part. And *remembering*, remembering to not Forget that Everything's All Right, when the evidence says exactly the opposite. How d'you let go of a rock in a river when the rock's the thing you're clinging to for friggin' *life*?"

"You let go," says the first voice. Inside, outside, a memory, an angel – it doesn't really matter where the words are coming from. "You let go, just as you suggested a moment ago, because when you do that, you are moving into the flow. That takes a great deal less energy than fighting. Ask and you will receive; but if you don't believe you'll receive, it becomes a little tricky: that makes for traffic jams, so it's rather difficult for the thing you're asking for to make it through the spaghetti junction you've built up all around you."

"You lead then, in future: it's a deal. OK?"

"Sure?"

"Yes, I'm sure."

Whatever name you, or I, might wish to give to a guiding intuition, a whisper of wisdom, the voice of the higher self, it comes from a force powerful and generous enough to sustain and support our lives and smile on our idiosyncrasies. We live in a Universe that is benevolent. It is set up to support us, not to thwart us: we're the only ones who do that.

Besides, there's something else: I've not thought about it much. But I've been noticing just lately that when I've been working with clients, I'm no longer alone. Not that we ever are, of course; but the presence of other energies has been palpable. There's been a feeling – a gently growing feeling – of powerful, loving beings standing behind me, above me. They move into my body: my hands and arms are moved in new and unfamiliar ways. And when this happens, magical things occur: chests expand, buttons almost burst.

"It feels like something has been opened up," says the person on the treatment table. And she reports back, or he does: his energy has soared; her marriage has softened; her boss has suddenly remembered how to smile.

Maybe, as I lie here, unable to do an outer *thing*, I shall find that some of those gifts-of-the-Gods will find their way home to me as well. Perhaps I've played Chiron the Wounded Healer just a little too long. There's one thing that's certain: I can't do things the old way any more. I can't *do* anything at all.

32

Metatron

So I've stopped. A broken back's a broken back's a broken back. I'm in shock and the mind-numbing pain carries me around the clock. But here's the thing: I'm *grateful*, I tell you, truly *grateful*.

"If you'd landed half an inch further down those steps," says John, "on the step with a steeper drop, it would have been a wheelchair job."

But no, I've still got legs that move and one day soon the body they're built to carry will work again. Bodies are good, even better than I realized. Heaven is right here on earth: I'll never doubt it again. Heaven makes it to earth through all kinds of bodies – through the trees, the flowers, the food, through *us*. So I'm resolved: I shall do everything in my power to love this sacred vehicle, right back into life.

It's hard work, I can't deny it. You lie around all day like an arthritic porpoise until eventually you heave your torso to a semi-upright slouch, and all the while you're knackered like you've just run to the moon and back. But weeks soon turn to months and – hey presto! – you find nearly a year has passed and you're feeling quite a lot improved. Maybe your back doesn't work the way it once did, but other things, like faith and trust and gratitude for life itself – well maybe they work a little better.

And something has changed: I know, now, that I'm not alone. I know that we're guided and held all the way. You'll see it when you believe it, they say, and I'm discovering that it's true. I can't do the doing so I'm doing the being instead. I've discovered the quietude which, if truth be told, and despite the efforts of the Great Kamakura Buddha and my other friends – I've really only read about before. I've found that it's a *good* thing.

I'm thinking about the story, the stories, and how we –

humanity, and each of us – don't need to run the old tapes any more. I'm thinking about light and colour, and how we can dissolve our illusions and surrender ourselves. We can transcend the limitations of our narrative; we don't have to be stuck in the mud. Surely that's the whole point? The energies of light show us that what we think is real is merely the illusion, the dream. We can wake up any time we choose, and create a new and better dream.

And I'm meditating – not every day, perhaps, but with far more consistency than I managed to find before. So one day the following spring, here I am, coming round from a nice snooze, in that half-awake-half-asleep chatting-to-the-angels kind of state, when all of a sudden I hear a voice.

"You can take the story out of the body," it says, "energetically."

This is no mere inner dialogue, it's not just a fraction of the kinds of conversations I've had with myself for years, like the ones *any* of us might have with ourselves any time, as we navigate our way through our days. No, this voice is coming from a foot-and-a-half in front of my wardrobe, approximately six feet north-east of my head – and that is where it will choose to place itself from now on. It's disembodied, rather like I was last year. I can't actually *see* anyone.

But this is not "you *can* take the story out of the body", this one sentence, as in 'here's an interesting idea why don't you try it some time'. This is more of a "go do it – and now is good." In other words, don't delay.

So I heave myself off to a quiet space – not to be disturbed – and I say,

"OK then. Show me what you want me to do."

And now it gets properly interesting.

I'm seeing, or sensing, an etheric kind of being, just above me – all bright light and golden instruments. I'm being shown a whole selection of beautiful coloured rays of light, quite different from any that I've seen before. They are iridescent, opalescent, pearly, pastel; and there are seven of them. I'm being directed to a scene now, a memory if you like, that has been held in my body, well away and out of sight. It has to do with Mr Outward Bound, as it happens, and I've not seen him for well over a decade. As far as I knew until that moment, any residue of that little connection was dealt with and dusted off years ago.

So I'm taking instructions. This etheric being is showing me how to lift this scene right out of my body, gently but without equivocation. It's quite wonderful to watch it leave; ah, but here is the real shock: as it departs, in comes Mr Outward Bound himself and takes up a position somewhere on the ceiling. He is transforming before my startled eyes. It wouldn't be an exaggeration to say he's beaming love and light right down at me.

Now that *is* a surprise.

So I send a message to my friend Clare:

"There's something happening here and I think you need to come and find out about it."

"How about now?" comes the reply, 30 seconds later.

Clare comes right around and we get to it. We take *all* the stories out of her body, one at a time; well that's a figure of speech. Fortunately, the stories go on and on as long as we're here on earth: without a storyline, wherever would we be? And now Clare takes quite a few of the stories out of my body too.

And who's arriving in the country tomorrow? Melissie! Thank God for that.

"Please come quick," I tell her. "Something extraordinary is happening here."

By the time Melissie arrives, I've already learned something else. The etheric being who has been showing me things appears to have the name Metatron. I can't do a lot to explain this in any way that would stand the test of reason. I've sensed colours and shapes; I've heard a name spoken: between them, the symbols and sounds amount to a clear sense of a mighty Archangelic force. I don't question it too deeply; I just know that it's a fact and it's really not negotiable.

I've vaguely aware that this being features in Melissie's work: there's even an angel spray with Metatron's name on it. For the time being, the fact that the bottle of my Hawaiian dream is widely known as the Metatron bottle has slipped my attention entirely. Within the small, constricted space of my mind, I know nothing about this Archangel at all. But very little of this mind-blowing experience has anything to do with the rational part of my brain.

Things are moving faster now. We work intensively for days, Melissie and I. We're story-free; we've never *been* so squeaky clean, so feathery light.

"By the way," she says. "Did you know there are seven new rays coming in?"

Yes I did, and this is what they're like. Yes quite, she says: different energy; new quality entirely. There's nothing new in the universe, of course; the only thing that changes is our ability to let things in. We live on opposite ends of the planet, this friend and I, and we've been receiving the same information at the same time; we're working hand in hand. And she knows that this new *thing*, this gift from the angels, must shift: it must spread its seed and grow, to reach the people who need it every bit as much as we do – maybe more. It's the how-to, the missing piece; the one I've been looking for ever since I found myself without a job. She takes it to her colleagues. She tells them all about it.

The phone starts ringing. Will I run a workshop here, a workshop there? Will I show people how to do this for themselves? Will I return to training others in the healing arts – as I'd done in a different way so long ago?

It feels a little soon: should I really move so far so fast? I'd better check in with my friends in the ethers, I reflect, and see what needs doing; how exactly it is meant to look. I must find out what exactly it is that they're asking me to do.

Step by step, a method is revealed: in the first instance, the workshop is to be given as a series of Attunements, followed by a series of energy Transmissions. There will be seven of each, to tune us all in to each of those divine rays – and clearance work, lots of it. And this, they say, is only the beginning.

The first workshop is approaching fast. They know me well, these sprites: just to make sure I don't start running around, or reading other people's books in the attempt to get it 'right', they put me into a high fever and start telling me the rest of the story – not the one I'm assisting people in digging out: I don't even want to *go* there. No, we can leave all that behind, all of us: the real story is the one that will replace the worn-out conditioning of the past. It even has the potential to change it…

Ah! Now you're talking.

They're telling me what's on offer as we surrender ourselves to a higher power, as we receive the gifts of spirit. But this is no mere idea; it's not just a concept: they have the method, the plan, and this will assist us mightily in the process. There's rather more to this than that first vital step of removing the story: much of it will unfold only gradually over the coming weeks and months.

"I hate to tell you, but we'll be needing you to make some new angel sprays," I tell Melissie as she prepares to board the plane.

"That's good."

So now I'm teaching, bringing this super-gift to share with super-people. Some of those who are asking me for this are quite familiar with energy healing work; I'm training them up to take one more tool out to their people. Others are looking for intensive healing for themselves. Either way, they're startled and amazed.

"I was stuck with that one for 25 years," says one of them. "ME or something. Thought I'd never be rid of it."

"I don't *believe* this!" says another. "That lump on my shoulder – it just got up and left. That depression – where did it go? Those panic attacks – they *dissolved*… Those, those, those…"

Variations on the sentiment are repeated through England, Scotland, through my beloved California. And now I'm in South

Africa again – right down at the root of the world. This gift they've given us is reaching people far and fast. It is changing lives from the inside out. First we are asked to remove the story; and now we're promised that our hearts will be opened, so that we find the courage and truth to do just that. Because the story fuels our identity, and the ego is none too keen to let us abandon this crucial food-source.

But then they go further, these angels: they offer to fill the vacant space with something larger, gentler, kinder, more creative.

"They're re-calibrating bodies," says Melissie, "so that we can hold more light. They're adjusting the settings, re-arranging our grids. And I think that all of this is what they've been trying to tell you about for a long time, since very early in your life. When they tripped you up on those steps, they didn't mean to hurt you anything like as much as it turned out. It was just that they had to find a way of halting your busy-ness, making you stop."

Ah, that would be it then. Yes, I'm OK with that. I'm not holding any grudges. And yes, I believe this is true: we are being re-calibrated. We're being taken apart, like that beautiful Japanese meal, returned to the palette; the heavy bits are being taken out so we can be re-assembled in greater harmony, greater joy and peace. A return to innocence: conscious innocence.

It makes perfect sense. This is awesome in its ramifications. We can change everything, if that is what we choose to do.

The months unfold. As they do so, the strange downloads that the angels have sent since the process began, the packages of energy and ancient knowledge, keep on coming in. I receive them as words, or as bodily sensations, randomly – sometimes by day, in meditation, sometimes by night when I expect to be asleep. They come as surges of immense heat, or waves of energy pulsing from the centre of my heart right through my arms and hands and out, or images of crystals implanted in my heart, or the purest pearly colours, shimmering, ardent and soft.

There are times when the input is so sudden or intense, so physical, that I understand why people have fantasies about alien abductions; why they fear that other beings on a different vibration may be hostile.

They are the very opposite, of course: they have come to our aid at a time of great change and need. So for much more of the time, as I receive their ongoing gifts, this is a gentle process, and very warm: I feel something like quantum packs of colour – of energy and information – entering my crown or my heart, and filtering through to the cells even of my fingers and toes. And I trust to time: the quantum packs will release their energy and information piece by piece, as the need arises through the months ahead.

But let's not forget about that angel-child of mine, the one that was left for dead. What about that miracle-person, Magdalen, because the real story, the one that mattered, began with her adventure from hell. How is she?

Metatron has worked on her, of course: like all of us, she has been letting go of her story too, keeping only the pieces that empower her. It's what she has done from the start: fourteen long years ago and more, she set her intention to carry on as though nothing had happened.

Early in this new process, almost as soon as this Archangelic gift arrived, she asked if she might attend a workshop. She joined in with all the others, asking for 'Metatronic' aid in removing the parts of the story she'd done with. They worked deeply with her and as she left the workshop, her eyes were bright and clear, her aura squeaky clean like the others. She felt restored, renewed, softer and safer as she set off for South Africa, to pour bottles and enjoy the sun.

And then came the next angel-tweak, a big one. In retrospect it begins to look as though the whole journey has been overseen by that super-Archangel Metatron, because in the wake of that workshop, with some of the traumas and fears shaken loose, a friend of Melissie's has now been called in. He practices Shiatsu and he's been working on her leg. As he does so, she has what she describes as a sudden vision: she sees the possibility of being able to bend her foot and place it firmly on the ground. This is not the way things generally work for her; her scepticism is way up with the best of her peers. I'm the one that does the weird stuff, not her.

I am at work but the phone is ringing; something prompts me to excuse myself and pick up. "Hey Mum! I just felt something funny in my foot – I was walking on the beach. I looked down and it had straightened out. I can get my shoe on; it's not hurting any more!"

Now to the average person, a little cramping foot that's straightened out, carrying a body that's limped its way through a decade and a half, may seem like something quite trivial. But it's not. This is merely the most obvious outer symptom, the last extremity, of an outer and inner struggle that has been nothing short of epic. No wonder my daughter has gone and bought herself a pair of the most precarious-looking high-heels you ever saw. She has gazed longingly through the windows of shoe shops for most of her conscious life: now she can walk tall.

The journey goes on – ours, and yours too – and we never need be stuck in anything, anywhere. We heal and we learn to love; that's why we're here. We're learning to love like the angels love, like God loves – with our hearts wide open, not from that old place of fear and need. We create the next steps of our journey through the way that we think and feel. We re-create the past, too, as we modify it gently, one step at a time. But there's really only one place to be, and that's here; there's only one time to be, and that's now. We carry our homes with us: they're right there in our hearts.

As the angels bring their light-beams in and promise to remove our story, they've promised to switch our hearts on; they've promised to point us on to that road we lost: the one that leads us back from fear to love. I have been told that if we wish to evolve, we need to call in the help of the angels, because in some way, they have been there too. They have been through their own journey of enlightenment, so they know how to get there; they know how to rescue us from ourselves.

Now that's some promise indeed.

So what can we learn from Metatron, and how does the system work? My friend Carina has rejoined me on my travels: she has some more questions to ask. She and I have come to know each other better now, and her questions are an attempt to make sense of the story that I, for one, have lived. But in that process, these questions make sense of many other stories too.

Nobody betrays us: we only betray ourselves. There are no accidents: there are only learning experiences. Come and share Carina's questions and feel your way into the possible answers for yourself, for the questions you have also asked, or wished to ask, in your own life, as we walk among the golden leaves of the early autumn sunshine. She and I are on that beloved West Coast of America. We're in the Redwood forests, on the way to Mount Shasta, one of my favourite places on the planet. I call it the Home of the Gods. You, of course, can be anywhere you like.

Five

Angel: a spiritual being acting as an attendant
or messenger of God, represented as being of
human form with wings

The Zohar calls Metatron "the Youth", identifies him
as the angel that led the people of Israel through the
wilderness after their exodus from Egypt,
and describes him as a heavenly priest.

33

Metatronic Healing

"You can take the story out of the body. This is where we start."

"Oh no no no!" says Carina. "You can't take away the story," she continues. "It's the story that makes you who you *are*."

"But it doesn't," I reply. "It makes you who you *were*: yesterday, last week, last year, living with all that stuff – the doldrums, the worries, the poverty, the grief. Is that what you want to keep re-creating? Because you can, if you like – or else you can have heaven on earth. But it *is* your choice."

"But in heaven all the interesting people are missing," says Carina. "That's what Nietzsche said, didn't he?"

We're looking up through the cathedral spires of the Sequoia trees at the azure dish beyond. The bark is thick and soft, the leaves evergreen and lush: the tallest trees in the world have their roots deeply planted in the earth, but they're reaching up to heaven with the most direct intent, closer to it than any cathedral spire.

"Yes," I reply, "and all kinds of clever minds around the planet are right there with him. All that love and light and blandness would be insufferable, they think: boring. I take their point. The villain of the piece is often far more interesting than the good guy, the sweet one with the pink cheeks and neat hair. But we could do with a bit of that peace in this crazy world."

All of us: we crave peace, abundance, joy, security, love; yet we love the dark stuff, we're constantly intrigued and seduced by it. The Prince of Light and the Prince of Darkness are duelling all the time, around us, inside us. It's what makes life interesting, the stories so compelling. The duels and conflicts create the stories, the songs and the dance.

"The villain, the Wicked Witch – it's all the same stuff, isn't it?"

says Carina. "We carry it around with us."

"Yes, it's just the ego. The ego loves the soap operas: they're the stuff of our identities, and the more sense of identity we have, the more separate we feel: bigger than, sadder than, smarter than, and all the rest of it. They make us individual, our little dramas; they put us right 'in' to the 'divide'. The ego turns double somersaults to keep us small: feed it with all your little sagas, then, your stubbornly limited beliefs, and it keeps right on going."

"Why are we so often drawn to the darkness, even when it disturbs us or upsets us?" Carina asks.

"Because of the darkness we hold inside *ourselves*! We don't like to look too closely at that. It's more comfortable to look outside – at the movies, or the feature articles, or the other people, or the news. It saves us that nasty feeling of wriggling in our seats. We prefer to leave the darkness inside us – but it *doesn't* just sit there. It churns around; it grows like fermenting dough. Then it takes a key part in running the show, the one that plays out as our lives.

"But you know what? Darkness itself isn't really the problem. In fact, it gives us great creative tools, if we get friendly with it. Darkness is the soil that germinates the seeds. It's the softness of sleep and the inspiration of our dreams. It's plush and fertile, the stuff of everything we use to sculpt our reality –most of our creations come from that hidden, unconscious place. God may have created light and found it good; but what did He create it from? The darkness is the mystery, the Source, the beginning. It's the womb of creation. But we are frightened of it, because we push down into it the stuff we don't want to see."

"Like all our feelings of dread, or jealousy, or guilt. Yeah, it's true," she muses aloud. "I don't like to own up to those myself too much."

"Yet they're just emotions: they don't rule us, unless we let them do so because we're frightened of them. So the real problem is the fear itself. Our collective history is full of fear – and our personal history too – it's the stuff that ego gorges on. And here's a thing, you know: the ego actually *lives* in that history; it comes from the past, every time. Something bad happens – we're left hungry in our pram – and the ego logs it. Then something worse happens – teacher makes a fool of us in front of the whole class – and the ego logs it. 'I'll show them!' says the ego.

"Before you can say 'soap opera', the ego is making all its decisions based on the bad stuff that happened before. Which means the ego creates more bad stuff, which only goes to demonstrate to the ego that it has been *right* all along! Look at all that evidence, after all… Like attracts like.

"But which would you rather be: happy, or right? So is that what you want to create?" I'm asking Carina. "We can do tragedy; we can do comedy: which do you choose?"

"I know which one I'd like to choose," she says. "I don't seem to manage it as often as I'd like, though."

"Quite. Because that's how we live our lives. We get involved in the spectacles, with all the emotions that build up around them. The gravitational force of what seems to be happening pulls us right down into the mud. If we start to witness the drama, though, rather than take on the central role, or even the bit parts, we can enjoy the pleasure of something more comfortable. We could call it our 'seat in the Circle – or the Stalls'. But you know what? The moment that emotions take over again, running us on our anger and resentment and all the rest of it, we find ourselves back on the stage, right in the thick of it.

"The clear sight we had just went. We're victims again. But the director isn't on that stage, in the cast. He or she is outside it, deciding on the quality of the moments, and the outcome. He's free to direct as he chooses: tragedy, comedy, terror, faith – *bliss*? How about bliss! There's a far greater chance of that kind of detachment from a place in the stalls, or behind the back-stage curtains, than there is from centre-stage."

"Obviously we all think we'd prefer comedy," says my friend, "but then your story's been pretty interesting, you must admit."

"In parts, from time to time, but a lot of it has been quite dull. Grinding poverty and despair don't leave a lot of room for entertainment or inspiration. Every human story is interesting, one way or another; it has lots of ups and plenty of downs. But I will say this: the story isn't running me any more – or it's running me for much less of the time than it was in the past. That spells freedom, you know."

"That'd be good," says Carina, with feeling.

"Freedom seems to be the greatest thing these angels have promised us," I suggest.

"But without the journey – the difficult bits – what would we ever achieve?" she asks. "Look at you: it's the story that's led to all of this, the angelic healing you're so excited about. Would that ever have found its way through you if you'd been mostly having fun?"

"Probably not," I concede. "Definitely not, in fact. I agree, it's the whole point. It's what my narrative has been all about, in the end. We tend to create things out of the bad times, as often as the good ones – most people would say much more often. It's the way we've been wired up for at least a few thousand years. If we opt for a life path of struggle, it seems that the opportunities it offers for growth and expansion are considerably enhanced – against the opportunities of a beach bum."

"Next time, maybe?"

"Sure – I'll go for it… And you know what the scientists have discovered in the last few years: joy or happiness is a higher vibration even than love. Check that! It makes plants grow faster and lusher – it's got to do the same to us, once we dig out that ancient conditioning. So you see it doesn't have to be that old way: have a hard time here, get brownie points in heaven.

"Point is we create heaven here, once we stop stressing out about the past or the future and get connected with now. That means the body, being right there with the way we breathe tames our mind-games. It's only when we're here, now, present, that the other realms can really hold our attention – because they're here, now, too, it's just that we tend not to notice them."

"What is an angel anyway?" Carina asks. "We've seen pictures of them and read poets' words about them right down through the ages. Are you saying they're real?"

"All those people can't be wrong! It's a good question though. Artists and mystics have given wings and harps and things to angels and cherubs: they've suggested golden trumpets and shining faces.

"Maybe a quantum mechanic would describe an angel as high-frequency energy instead. He might be accused of taking away the magic and the mysticism but the bottom line is that he would be right. This *is* what they are, because that's what the Universe is – us too. We are energy; spirit is energy; everything is energy. And energy in any form moves, evolves and grows. As it moves, it shifts other things as well, like our own awareness, for instance."

"So you're saying that spirit beings are energy," Carina says. "D'you think that angels are energy that's kind of freed up; not tied in to a body, but otherwise more like us than we maybe thought?"

"Yes, I suspect that they're like us in certain ways – how else would they be so helpful to us? They're less visible than we are, of course, and they're way ahead of us in terms of understanding or awareness. But all energy is power; and it's all conscious.

"As we wake up, which is really another way of saying as our heart centres are activated, so we escape the grip of the ego and get to see the truth behind our illusions, we begin to transcend our stories. On the 'stage' we were just talking about, you're right in the thick of it so of course you don't see clearly. Once you get that 'seat in the Stalls,' or step back a bit, if you like, then you get more of a bird's-eye view. You see the threads, and you see why they're there."

"Why they're there? Are you saying there's always a reason for things, then? That's a proper New Age cliché, isn't it?"

"Yes. And a cliché gets to be a cliché because people keep finding it's true, so they keep saying it."

We're walking through the woods now, in silence; the caws and whistles of the Warblers and the gentle tapping of the woodpeckers are the only sounds for miles around. Light glistens through the morning dampness of the leaves; underfoot, all is soft.

The key to it all, it seems, to all that most of us ever want – like peace and faith and happiness and love – is opening the heart: easy to do in the simple beauty of nature that's all around us. In the trials of life, it's rather more difficult, which is why it's been the goal of every spiritual tradition on earth since time began. We're finding our way from our heads to our hearts. We're shifting our consciousness from the place where our egos hide and control us to the place where our souls shine a guiding light that has generally been just above our reach, just outside the visible spectrum, so to say.

The Sanskrit word for the heart centre is *hridaya*: it stands not for the physical heart but for a place of consciousness near the centre of the chest. The word means that there is a cosmic centre of Existence, Knowledge and Bliss, from which the whole universe arises: whether we're talking of a whole universe or of a single human being, this heart centre is the same.

Our physical hearts are not to be ignored, though.

"Hey, feel this," I ask Carina. "D'you mind if I try a little tapping, like those woodpeckers?"

"Go ahead," she says.

I tap her simultaneously on the back of her chest and the front, gently, slowly, for half a minute or so.

"Feel the energy in your heart. You know what? These amazing organs decide for themselves when life shall start and when it's time for us to hang up our boots. They feel, but they think too; they have brain cells of their own. Your heart will empower you if you let it. Breathe right into it, right now. Feel the energy in your heart."

"Hey!" says Carina. "That's neat."

"Well, get this. The massive energy-field around your heart reaches out to tap into and embrace the rest of the world.

"You know they say that if we wish to create anything of value, if we want something to work, we must really *mean* it; we must care about it, and feel the reality of it with all our hearts. Do you know why that's literally true? It's because that energy-field around these hearts of ours is 5000 times larger and stronger than the one that surrounds the brain. Five thousand times! Our heart centres, and our physical hearts themselves, deserve some respect.

"What's more, the angels are promising to assist us in removing the veil, in activating that centre so that it is consciously awakened as the wellspring of our spiritual and emotional lives."

"The angels, or this Archangel?" she asks. "Are we talking one angel, a team of them, what?"

"I'm describing these teachers as 'they'; and yet I'm feeling this great angel Metatron. It feels like a plural being, expressed through all these rays, all these different aspects of one great body of energy. I learned early that while these individual strands, which are really just individual aspects of a great body of light, work as a team, each of them can also do something different on its own."

"And the Metatron rays reach the heart, do they?" she asks.

"Yes really. And that's where parts of it get just a little bit like some of the older, more familiar energy healing methods," I tell her, "in the sense that the separate beams can be used as energies that fortify and nourish us, but rather more potent than those other systems. There seems to be pretty wide agreement among the people who are showing up on the courses, that these energies transcend those ones we've been more used to using in the past."

"So they kind of nourish you, do they, these energies?"

"Yes. You can feed these beautiful rays into someone, to restore them, to heal their bodies, to build up their confidence and their power.

"Each ray has its own quality, its own special job to do. Like us. And it's often a good idea to bolster a person with wholesome, fortifying energies – or food, if you like – before offering them the opportunity to let go of stories they may have been attached to for decades. The first message was to lift out the story – only the outworn bits, of course – and the Metatronic energies give us plenty of support for that process; plenty of back-up. But that removal of old stuff is really only the start of something that's radically life-changing, life-enhancing."

"It's a strange name, Metatron," says Carina.

She's right; it's unusual for an Archangel: almost all the others end in 'el'. Meta means going beyond and tron means matrix. So the name means something like "beyond the matrix; beyond the template for our physical life that we can grasp and understand." But 'tron' may also come from 'thun', which means 'being'. So the name of this great Archangel also means something like 'super being'.

There's only one other angel with that kind of a name: he's called Sandalphon, and the legends tell us that they were twin brothers long, long ago, when they were human. Metatron brings the heaven energy down to us here on earth, they say; Sandalphon keeps us here, safely protected and grounded.

"I don't know about you," I say, "but speaking for myself I'm really quite happy to do without any more stories that are sad or bad in my own life. In the end most of our stories are ones that we've told ourselves; they're fictions we've dreamt up as we've done our best to navigate our way through life. I'm suggesting to my ego that she take a back seat. But don't let anyone ever kid you that they've found the answers: that's the danger of religion. If we're still on the planet, we're still learning: we're learning through our stories, and we're letting go of bits of them along the way. That's certainly why *I'm* on the planet. It's why you're on the planet."

"It's why you love movies," says Carina.

"Yes, I love the stories, the movies, the books. I get caught up in the action when something in the scene touches on what's mine; it pushes my buttons; it reminds me of a joy or a pain keenly felt. My emotions come in – or out – and I'm in there with the drama. As time goes on, though, I'm more interested by the craft and less caught up with the story. I'll give myself that much credit."

"So if it all happens for a reason, there are no accidents, no betrayals, it seems the whole thing is more like a script – this thing we call life."

Yes, I really do believe that.

"Belief is far too tame a word, though. I know it, with a certainty that comes from somewhere very deep: it's a knowing that's right in the cells of my bones. We set up pre-birth planning meetings. We take advice from our guides about what we will come here to learn or sort out, and then we set to and write the scene. Which means we ask old friends, or brothers, or mothers – or whoever – to play a role that will help us to do just that."

"Like, betray you, you mean?" asks Carina, "or take you to the frozen north. Lose all the money your parents gave you to build your home. Or break all their promises and chuck you on the street with all your kids, jobless. Or come and smash their car into you when you're six."

"Exactly," I agree. "Or even more to the point, we'll say to those very people, 'I've got this little thing I need to do, which means I'll have to get badly damaged when I'm very young. Please will you be my mother? You're just the person I need. You'll get huge rewards in the end, I promise. Or 'please will you be my betrayer?' Whatever it is you know you're going to need."

"That's heavy," says Carina.

"Yes and no. It's heavy from where we stand in our bodies and emotions. If we're coming from our souls, I'm pretty confident that it looks rather different."

"Like we're doing each other a service."

"Yes really. So you may say to someone you've known for aeons, 'hey, I've really got to get over a shocking habit I caught some time ago, handing over my responsibility, all my power, to other people: the church, the man. Please will you set me up to believe in you and then dump me? Because if you do that, I'll have no choice: I'll have to get it that I'm the authority in my own life. Or 'will you be the scariest father on the planet, the mad mother, the primary teacher from hell?' You name it – you make the choices."

"So you're saying that every time, there's something in it for you, or me – the person doing the asking?"

"It's always an exchange of some kind. It just doesn't feel that way when you're being asked to contemplate something impossible or very painful, so you, or your friend that you're recruiting, will probably say, 'no, please no – I love you far too much to do that. I can't face the thought of hurting you so much, or seeing you hurt so much, or being hurt'."

"So 'up there' we're all good friends," says Carina.

"Exactly, so you'll probably say 'no really: I need you to do that. If you do that for me, I'll step right back into the power I lost some time back in the Middle Ages. Or I'll help my Mum and all her friends to find faith: proper faith, the kind that flouts the False Evidence Appearing Real. Or I'll develop compassion; patience; tolerance; wisdom – anything you like."

"That puts a new spin on a few things in *my* family," Carina comments drily.

"It always does. And it gets less heavy, because the past often isn't what you thought it was at all. The people you thought you detested have loved you *so* much they've even let you hate them so you would be free to get on and do your thing."

"So that's why we need the story?" Carina says. "We wrote it so we'd learn our lessons."

"That's right, and we stay with the story – or with any one chapter of it – as long as we're still learning the lesson that goes with the chapter. But you know how things get toxic when they're past their sell-by date? It may be a story, it may be a piece of cheese – either way, it turns to mould... So it's a good idea to flush it out."

"And all these people who are supposed to love us, while they go on the rampage with their ego trips: how about Mr Outward Bound? Does this even apply to him?"

"Yes."

"And Gabriel?"

"Oh him especially. He taught me all about colour and set me up and then whisked it all away – but only on an earthly level. Behind the scenes there's a different agenda. I'm walking in the desert for years in the wake of it, it's true. But it's when we're pushed to our limits and beyond that the other stuff happens, like meeting the angels! And what the angels do, as they beam in with their divine surgery and remove the story, is they restore the matrix. They restore us to that place of real, full self-responsibility, because what happens as we ground ourselves in these bodies of ours is we get caught right up in the story. We forget who we really are."

"Who are we, then? What are we?"

"We're love: that's all we are – pure unconditional love; we're innocence and we're light. Try telling that to a terrorist – or to me when I'm flying home in a Boeing 707, jobless and fit for the knackers' yard: you'll wish you'd kept your mouth shut. But it's true, we plan it all. We can tweak the details as we go along, but in essence we write the script in advance.

"Then what the angels do, when we reach the moment when we're ready for it, is they restore us to our original state of innocence, but now it's conscious innocence, so we're not victims any more.

"We can step into alternative realities from the one that we're in: whether it's the Kabbalah or a quantum mechanic telling you so, it doesn't make a lot of difference. This is the truth, whatever the rationale that explains it. Take out the story and you do step out of one reality into a fresh one."

"So then you forgive them, all those people? And you forgive yourself?"

"Yes, except that there's nothing to forgive anyway. There can't be, since we're responsible for our own creations."

"That's a big one," she says. "But I guess it makes sense, if you get your head around it."

"Your heart, more like."

"Yes, perhaps. Why does the ego get such a bad press in all of this? Isn't an ego – a sense of being a somebody – exactly what we need, to do this life journey at all – to survive, even?"

"Yes, that's got to be why it's wired up that way: the ego can be our greatest ally but of course it can be our greatest enemy instead, especially while we're embroiled in the illusions that all our dramas create; the feeling of being separate and isolated and so on."

"But it seems to me," she says, "that people on a spiritual path are sure the ego's bad and wrong. Suppress it; push it down, get it out of the way, they say. Does that work? Is that how we get to enlightenment or a life that works?"

"No," I agree. "That's not it. The ego gets a bad press because we've all seen what happens when it gets out of balance: the likes of Hitler have shown us that for centuries, millennia even."

"And it's easier to see what's happening with other people's egos than our own."

"Right. It's all smoke and mirrors. What we're really scared of is our own darkness. But really, the ego is just an energy body too, and every body of energy wants to survive. No wonder it's scared of giving up its power, its place in the spotlight. It takes itself a bit seriously, perhaps; when survival is the name of the game, we all tend to put importance into being earnest or clever or funny. We want to be liked and validated and loved, or even just to convince ourselves we're OK. As the ego is part of our own survival strategy, just like you said, then this isn't really a lot to ask."

"No," says Carina. "Best to be friendly."

"And what the angels show us is to expand and embrace, not contract and reject. The angels know how to do life with a light touch. So if we embrace the ego gratefully, as a part of ourselves and as the vehicle that transports us through life, it enables us to be here and get around and do our thing. It takes us out into the world, into the place where we need to be.

"And here's the big step; the big gift," I add. "When we surrender to that bigger thing – the heart, with its hotline straight to the soul – then the ego, which on the whole has been lonely and frightened and, like all of us, wants nothing more than to be loved, can merge into this warm, expansive place. It gets bigger, it grows into the parts of us that can *fly*. That's a win-win. Of course we have to do that, we have to open our hearts, if we want to make it through the next few decades, things being what they are. It's not negotiable: the planet's letting us know that, in no uncertain terms."

"Which is part of why loads of people are waking up," says Carina, "being kicked awake by the Universe."

"Yes, or by their own higher selves. But there's even more here that goes on with the heart," I enthuse. "It's very amazing. You know what? A happy heart literally, *physically* or energetically makes everyone else happier and healthier too: it acts like a tuning fork, entraining the people around us into greater happiness and better health: you only have to hang out for a while with someone whose heart centre is in good shape and you feel a whole load better too."

"We know that intuitively, don't we?"

"Yes – and the scientists have shown it happens actually. A healer with a balanced heart brings a client's heart-field into line with his own: it lowers the patient's blood pressure and all kinds of wonderful things."

"Seems like the heart really is the heart of the matter!" says Carina.

"That must be why artists have always in some sense been our guides on this planet: the music people, the painters, the poets. They have pulled divine inspiration straight through into their hearts. They've done their best to raise the vibrations, their own as well as others', since time began. With the aeons and aeons of fear that have built up behind us, though, the stuff we've inherited from the people before, who got it from the people before, opening our hearts has not been an easy thing to do."

"But you really believe that Metatron is offering something tangible here, don't you? Something tangible that literally wakes our hearts up?" Carina asks seriously.

"I know it. I'm seeing the evidence of it all the time. Metatron brings us the gentlest of surgery – spiritual surgery. All you feel is a wonderful sense of joy, and warmth, and expansion. You get bigger, emotionally, spiritually, mentally even. It's not uncommon that people even feel their chests expand. They start breathing again, as though they'd just discovered this magical stuff called fresh air. And then he gives us soul food. This really is something tangible – or sense-able at any rate. So you can *take heart*, can't you? The heart is the coeur, the place where your courage lies. It will work for everyone if we get these hearts of ours running along nicely. Metatron is offering us all of this."

"So you lose the story, or rather the story loses its grip of you, and you get to keep hold of yourself - right? Your heart has the space to grow and stretch. In fact, you could even watch that play and you'd begin to feel then that the hero, or the heroine, is pretty OK after all," she suggests.

"Yes yes, you step right into your Self – the Self with the big S. You get to keep the learning, the wisdom, the joy, of course you do. It's only the soap opera that gets up and leaves: the thick emotions, the grungy anger, the hatred and angst and frustration and jealousy and all the rest of it – all the stuff that feeds the identity and puffs up the ego into its false power. You feel quite different."

"Cool," says Carina.

"No, warm," I reply. "Because remember that you're not only getting to keep the useful stuff – all the good bits – you're growing a whole lot stronger in all kinds of ways. Taking out the story is only the beginning of the process: what's to come is downloads of the most fabulous light. What was it that the lovely Archangel Gabriel said to Mary: 'Behold, I bring you tidings of great joy: you are about to give birth to the divine power within yourself; the one that's been hiding away all these years.' Something like that anyway."

"Gabriel again…"

"Yes! The best messenger of all."

"What happens in the workshops, then? How's it done, the activating of the heart centre?" she asks.

"They attune different stations around your body to pick up the energy that Metatron sends through, then they use their light rays to open up people's hearts and pour the power in – the divine power."

"Through you?"

"Through me, or whoever is doing the teaching that day. First, we touch each person on the forehead, or the hand, or wherever that Attunement is to be focused; that's like adjusting the radio to receive certain wavelengths. Then people tuck themselves up comfortably on the floor, with a blanket and pillow, and Metatron sends through an energy Transmission – the first of seven. More later, of course – but seven the first time."

"What does it feel like, a Transmission? What does it do?"

"It transmits a pure, potent energy straight into your heart. Some people respond to it by falling asleep; others feel a sense of bliss. Sometimes people cry a little: there's all kinds of different things that happen with it. The only thing that matters is that from then on this energy is available to them – to use for themselves, and to call on for others in the healing work they do. It's *divine*, this energy, in the true, original sense. It seems to begin the process where lives really start to be changed.

"In the first workshop, there are seven Transmissions in all. In later ones – where a different quality of energy comes in, metallic or crystalline for instance – there are more. And these are interspersed with practical sessions where in the early workshops we clear the story – with individuals or with whole groups. In later stages of the work we bring in the different rays to use in all kinds of ways: sometimes for specific physical benefits; other times for more emotional or spiritual support."

"How are the clearances done?" she asks.

"There's a formula that we've been given and now developed quite neatly. We find that with all this divine energy in place, removing the story is easy. It's quite effortless for a person to move into a beautifully relaxed state of mind; easy to be guided to see the places in your body where your stories have been lodging in the dark. The Metatron 'team' – this is the best description I can find for those gentle strands of luminescent, shimmering energy I told you about – makes itself available; in fact it wouldn't be an exaggeration to say that they penetrate the body tissue and work together to lift the old story – the one that's way past its sell-by date – right out. And that's where the essences come in, because bodies like to have a *thing*, remember, to work with.

"Bodies know that light is the essence; it's the life force. They know that light carries information. So when we bring those high-vibration coloured essences and give their support to a body that's trying to let go of some kind of trauma or memory which may be quite ancient, the body understands the message held within the colour and translates it into energy that it can use. And you know that expression, how something happens at 'lightning speed' – well that's what happens here. Bring in the actual,

215

physical essence to the business of clearing out a story and it vanishes in a flash. That really *is* cool."

"So that's why this system works so closely with Colourworks?" asks Carina.

"They're the same thing, really. Melissie and I are tuning into much the same places in the network, or the universal energy grid, from opposite ends of the planet and we're running twin systems. They work best of all together."

"Do people always have to go on a workshop to get this kind of healing?"

"They go on a workshop if they want intensive healing: the Transmissions are a life-changing gift to anyone. But you can simply go for a treatment to someone who's trained if you want to leave behind a specific life-event: a trauma of some kind, or an addiction, for instance. How you work with this depends what you're looking to do."

What great hopes this offers us all as we set about the work we have to do, forgiving here, taking responsibility there, claiming or reclaiming our divine power and light, doing the thing we're here for.

Take out the story, the drama, the stuff you no longer need, and you step into a different reality entirely. Remove the story and you find that the charge around a chapter of your life has lost its force; you discover the detachment you've maybe needed for years. Change your *opinion* around an event and the outcome is essentially changed.

As the work with Metatron develops, we are finding that this possibility of altering what has gone before goes deeper and further than merely changing our opinion about it, and the emotions we may feel as a result of this. This great Angelic power has shown us that we can revisit the past – sometimes the deep past; other existences; other journeys.

We can enter a scene and take a close look, so that we can discover the source of a recurring pattern of behaviour or addiction; we can pinpoint just what the problem has been. We can find the cause behind the cause.

So we watch this scene, just as you would watch a movie. But then we wind the movie backwards, like a film sequence where a banana is zipped up, or a plant retracts into the soil. We rewind the reel, and through techniques of energy breathing and visualization, we support the person in taking back their power. Then they can re-enter the scene, but from an empowered place; they're free now to choose a different outcome.

They do this, they return to the present moment, and they come out profoundly altered. This is one of the methods we use; we find that the past can be changed in a way that is so close to tangible it's nothing short of miraculous.

We're the authors and the directors of our lives. We write the script and we oversee the production. The exciting discovery here, though, goes beyond this: it is that we can *re*-write the script, we can impact it backwards, so to speak. We can create a new and improved version of our life story. Whew.

We can change the past...! The inkling of that preposterous truth that came to me in the funfair turns out to be true. It's even been scientifically verified.

"And then we go even further," I tell Carina. "If you can handle any more..."

"Like?"

"Take out the story and that leaves a space. Now they can pour in something different from before; they can filter new information into the cells. It's like telling your cells to buck their ideas up so they create a better life."

"What, like change the DNA, you mean?"

"That's how the scientists would describe it, yes. And that means you change things for previous generations and future ones."

"Hey that's quite a claim," she says.

"I'm not claiming it, I'm just suggesting it. The scientists have already found we switch our genes on and off according to the things we focus on, the way we think and so on.

"They're realizing that we get to change our children's gene pool by whatever we happen to put in during a lifetime. Don't you think it makes sense, change the story, change the thinking; change the thinking, change the whole thing."

"I do get that it's about our consciousness. It puts a huge responsibility on us."

"And huge freedom," I remind her. "They're two sides of the same coin."

"But it's awesome!" she says. "I'm really getting it now. You change the cellular programming and that means you get to change the past, kind of on a physical level – like a more inter-generational level of what you've been watching all these years, as your daughter has reclaimed her body? Do you mean clear the memory and then you're free to re-write the story in a different version? And you really mean you can free up your *ancestors*?"

"That's pretty much the way it works. Heal the ancestors, heal the kids, heal the family tree. Heal the heart, heal the family, heal the world. There's past lives too: you can change the outcome of deep-past events, so then you change the quality of your own response because you've altered the conditioning that you bring into this life with you.

"And how about clearing our spaces – environmental spaces? They are part of our reality, just as much as our stories, our loved ones, our health, our friends; the land and the houses that hold us need sorting out just as much as we all do. But we'll get to that later."

Carina needs some quiet time. She's been absorbing a good dose of new information. But she has a few last questions: "How about 'Dorothy's' other friends, your other two kids? How are they doing?"

"Oh, the unsung super-heroes of the piece: Courage and Wisdom. They're doing great. The younger one is in the City in

London, wisely creating heaven on earth – in a tangible way. The other, my first-born, she does all kinds of things. Right now she works mostly with young offenders: drug rehabilitation treatment and training. She's thinking of coming to work with me."

"And your home – where's your home these days? That place down the coast – is that it?

"It's one of them. We come and go. London here, America there. A bit of Africa. It doesn't make a lot of difference in the end. It's that tortoise thing: we make our home anywhere, so long as we bring our hearts along too."

"Like Dorothy."

"Exactly. What she found was she'd never left home in the first place.

"It's an oddly tricky journey we all seem to travel, just to find some place that's been right there all the way along."

- - - - - - - - - - - -

Before enlightenment, we chop wood, carry water: we do the relationship, pay the bills, wash the floor, repair the car. As a hint of enlightenment begins to dawn on our horizons, or in our hearts, there may not be too much on the outside that seems to have changed; by and large we do the same things as before: we wash the dishes, dig the garden, feed the kids, mend the shirt.

But there's a subtle shift: that growing shaft of light brings a touch of present-moment awareness into the actions; and then some more. The quality we bring to these things, the way that we do them: all of this begins to change. And *that* makes all the difference.

Humanity has been full of courage lately – taking giant steps in raising its awareness, literally lifting its vibrational frequency to a higher place, a more conscious state of being. The scientists are telling us that the earth itself has more or less doubled its frequency in recent years. We're doing the same thing.

We've expanded our vision. That's why we've been able to say yes to these new rays. There's nothing new in the universe, of course, except for us: we're the ones who get renewed.

Light is more than welcome - it's needed – all over this brave planet. And the light that comes straight to us from the angels is the clearest light of all.

Heaven is out there, all right, and it's in here too. Spirit, matter, the gods, the angels, us – ultimately it's all the same stuff. Even the trees and the flowers, the earth and the rocks; that's all condensed spirit too: all of it is alive. The difference between one form and another has mostly to do with the level of frequency on which it vibrates, but all of it has a consciousness, a heart.

And we all have our roles, our individual parts to play in the unfolding drama; the real drama. I'm not talking about little stages here, more the big one – the stage of life, the universe, our very purpose for being here at all.

As we embrace our path and walk our truth, we release the seed of our own unique aspect of Divinity and take responsibility for who we are. We must each shine our own light. God is the power, certainly, but we are the light bulbs, and every one of those is needed. Like Christmas tree lights, when one bulb goes the whole thing packs up. We're all in this together. We each have to stand up and do our part, the one we opted for in the first place. Hiding our light away does no-one any favours, not us or them. So if we want change, we have to work as a team. There's really no other way. We're only in human form for a while. We're given time – let's use it the best way we can.

As for the angels, they've always been here and they always will. Maybe we're ready to get to know these light beings a little better; and as we come to know them, they can help us to know ourselves. As we understand ourselves, we shall expand into the power of our Selves, to create what's good, to maintain what works, to destroy what we no longer need.

Maybe that's why Metatron's influence is so apt just now, as we're expanding into the 21st century through this time of exponential change.

The legends say that Metatron led the people of Israel out of Egypt and into the Promised Land. They say he is so vast he embraces the whole of the earth. They even say that he builds a bridge between earth and heaven itself.

There's more to it, of course – the healing that's coming from Metatron is moving on to deeper and higher levels. But that will do for now: for the time being the angels are done here, in these pages; and so am I.

God bless you, and I wish you only the very happiest of stories.

Note

To respect the privacy of the people involved, some of the names in the text have been changed. Certain small details and parts of the chronology have been marginally altered for the purposes of reading quality; but in essence the story is fact not fiction. The exception is Carina, whom I have never met: at the time of writing she was placed in the future. She is a composite of a number of friends, students and clients, all of whom have asked the most

---

Would you like to know:
- How you are influenced by the colours in your environment?
- What your personal colour preferences tell you about who you are and what you need?
- How to use colour for greater health, balance, peace of mind?
- How to harness your true colours for authentic, soul power?

Then visit us at www.color4power.com for your free colour gifts:

- Colour Psychology and Healing – a beautifully illustrated e-book
- Soul Rays – an audio for peaceful relaxation
- Foods from the Sun: a Guide to Joyful Eating – illustrated e-book

---

helpful questions as the process has unfolded before our eyes. I like Carina enormously, so who knows? Maybe before much longer our paths will cross...

And Thank You

It goes without saying that I acknowledge with the deepest gratitude and warmest thanks all of the people in whose company I have walked parts of this journey. They include, most obviously, my children and my husband, and all of my extended family and friends. They include the entire cast of the text: my teacher Gabriel; William Grey-Campbell who reads the stars; Edwin Courtenay who reads the very depth of your soul; and many others not mentioned in the text who gave me so much of themselves. They include Dr Kim Jobst in England and Suzanne Mendelssohn in New York, both of whom have given me constant encouragement and belief. They include, of course, Melissie Jolly who has walked with me and incidentally read every page of the text, screaming for more as it spilled out rather chaotically through the autumn of 2007, and other early, helpful readers and critics such as Clare Glennon and Paddy Yorkstone. They include Moira Bush, Korani Connolly, Elizabeth Jones, and Ian and Sue Etchells.

They include angels and wizards far too numerous to list, which means, of course – as the dedication has already acknowledged – all the floaty people.

There are two people, however, that I must thank over and above all of this. Michael Skipwith, my friend, healer and guide of 25 years, has stood behind me and filled me with courage, urging me on and working to promote actively whatever I may have to share. And Carlo Constandinou, my other miracle-worker and spiritual counsellor: before the Archangels walked into my life, he had already brought much of Magdalen's life force back into her body and her spirit, and some years later he told me I must write this book, editing the earliest version voluntarily, from the clarity of his heart and mind. I would never have dared or presumed to chronicle the events of my less-than-brilliant career, but he's not a man I'd mess with: if he speaks, I act.

Do You Want to Know More?

Pippa Merivale teaches and practices Colourworks and Metatronic Healing in London, the UK and internationally. She is available for private sessions at the College of Psychic Studies in Kensington (www.collegeofpsychicstudies.co.uk). There is also a growing body of teachers and practitioners for both of these healing systems, which work closely together.

For general information about colour healing, Colourworks, Metatronic Healing and a range of books, e-books and audio resources, our twin websites, www.metatronic-life.com and www.color4power.com are works in progress.

If you'd like to come on a workshop, you will find information about the courses, and the dates and the locations.

If you would like to invite a Colourworks or a Metatronic teacher to give a talk or a workshop in your area then please write to us: pippa@color4power.com or pippamerivale@yahoo.co.uk If you just want to share your experiences with us, then please do. We can't promise to answer every message, but we get to as many as we can, and we'll be delighted to hear from you anyway.

If you wish to find a therapist, the database is growing: you may well find there's someone practising in an area not too far from where you live.

If you would like to know more about Colourworks, you will find information about this too, on the website, along with links to the team. Here are the links:

www.colourworks.org

www.korani.net and www.moirabush.com

Metatronic Healing and Colourworks work closely together: as Metatron has said, "It's the same thing anyway."

BOOKS

O is a symbol of the world, of oneness and unity. In different cultures it also means the "eye", symbolizing knowledge and insight. We aim to publish books that are accessible, constructive and that challenge accepted opinion, both that of academia and the "moral majority".

Our books are available in all good English language bookstores worldwide. If you don't see the book on the shelves ask the bookstore to order it for you, quoting the ISBN number and title. Alternatively you can order online (all major online retail sites carry our titles) or contact the distributor in the relevant country, listed on the copyright page.

See our website www.o-books.net for a full list of over 400 titles, growing by 100 a year.

And tune in to myspiritradio.com for our book review radio show, hosted by June-Elleni Laine, where you can listen to the authors discussing their books.

mySpiritRadio